Rails West.

Rails West.

BY
GEORGE B. ABDILL

EASTERN MINNESOTA'S BUCOLIC CHARMS are captured in this lovely view of a glossy eightwheeler and five coaches on the Taylor's Falls line, built in 1880 by the Taylor's Falls & Lake Superior Railroad, assisted by the Minneapolis & St. Louis. Later operated by the St. Paul & Duluth, the scenic branch extending 20 miles between Wyoming and Taylor's Falls on the sparkling St. Croix River was purchased by the Northern Pacific in 1900 and abandoned in 1948. The picturesque road was a great favorite with pleasure-seekers and many excursions were operated over it.   (Courtesy of Northern Pacific Railway)

BONANZA BOOKS   NEW YORK

© MCMLX, SUPERIOR PUBLISHING COMPANY

ALL RIGHTS RESERVED

LIBRARY OF CONGRESS CARD NUMBER 60-14424

This edition published by Bonanza Books,
a division of Crown Publishers, Inc.,
by arrangement with Superior Publishing Company.

I J K L M N O P

PRINTED IN THE UNITED STATES OF AMERICA

Dedicated to the

BRAVE BREED OF MEN

who pioneered Western railroads

PREFACE

The conquest of America's great western frontier has provided writers with a fertile field, rich in color, drama, and action. In the vast region beyond the Mississippi the free mountain trapper roamed as wild as any savage, blue-clad troopers died in their Indian-ringed formations, and the buffalo hunters left a trail of bones in the wake of their heavy Sharps rifles. The bosoms of the waterways were furrowed by pioneer steamboat men, piloting their flimsy wooden paddlers up channels that had seen only the skin bull-boats of the natives and the bateaus of the fur brigades.

In this huge domain, stretching from the Father of Waters to the Pacific shores, transportation had always been a problem. Early trails led across trackless seas of prairie and waterless sands of burning deserts, over mountains where eternal snow brushed the clouds, and through forests and valleys lush with the miracles wrought by water. Each of these features presented obstacles to the traveller, but out of the East a solution to these problems was soon to appear.

Clattering along beneath a billow of white steam and smoke the Iron Horse rolled into the valley of the Mississippi, the symbol of the end of the wilderness days. In a few short decades this rattling, snorting mechanism would span the entire West with shining ribbons of rail, driving the buffalo, covered wagons, and even the palatial river steamers into obscurity.

This book, intended as a companion to THIS WAS RAILROADING and PACIFIC SLOPE RAILROADS, attempts to present a pictorial journey over the old railroads that spread from the Mississippi to the Pacific Ocean. The photographs selected depict the saga of American railroading in the West during the turbulent years of expansion, the days of iron men and wooden cars. Brief case histories tell the stories of some roads and the pictures embrace many others; if your favorite pike was a victim omitted through lack of space, the writer tenders his apologies.

The task and pleasure of assembling the photos would have been impossible without the generous assistance of the many who aided. The fabulous collections of Dr. S. R. Wood, Fred Jukes, Ronald V. Nixon, Ben W. Griffiths, Arthur Petersen, Herb Arey, Don H. Roberts, John Labbe, Roy D. Graves, David L. Joslyn, Gerald M. Best, and other lovers of trains have been heavily drawn upon, and to these goes the author's heartfelt gratitude, for they keep alive the golden memories of steam railroading.

Others who deserve special thanks include Chas. E. Fisher, president of the Railway & Locomotive Historical Society; Glenn H. Johnson, Jr., State Historical Society of Colorado; Mrs. Alys Freeze, Denver Public Library; Paul M. Bunting, St. Louis Southwestern Ry.; L. L. Perrin, Northern Pacific Ry.; N. J. Finigan, Canadian Pacific Ry.; James N. Sites and Lee Borah, Association of American Railroads; Al F. Zimmerman, Brotherhood of Locomotive Engineers and a fine railroad man; Ray Maxwell, Missouri Pacific Railroad; L. R. Smith, Asst. Gen. Mgr., and J. L. Bart, of the Texas & New Orleans Railroad; D. B. Jenks, President, and Esther M. Glasper, of the Chicago, Rock Island & Pacific Railroad; Allen Van Cranebrock, Burlington Lines; J. G. Shea and staff, Southern Pacific Company; M. R. Cring, Missouri-Kansas-Texas Lines; E. C. Shafer and staff, Union Pacific Railroad; Geo. J. Handzik, Atchison, Topeka & Santa Fe Railway; L. A. Brown, Wabash Railroad; R. L. Crandall, Rayonier, Inc.; Frank F. Perrin, Great Northern Railway; Priscilla Knuth, Oregon Historical Society; Illinois Central Railroad; Jack Slattery, Jack's Photo Service, Coos Bay, Oregon; Mrs. M. P. Hughes; Ben Baldridge; J. B. Shores, of the Texas & Pacific Railway, and others who aided in various ways. To each and every one of you, my sincere thanks.

I am deeply indebted to my publisher, Albert P. Salisbury, for his patient assistance in technical matters, and to my wife, Annette Abdill, for her cheerful inspiration and understanding.

TABLE OF CONTENTS

Chapter 1 — GATEWAY TO THE PACIFIC................................Page   11

Chapter 2 — THE CENTRAL PLAINS.................................Page   47

Chapter 3 — SOUTH BY SOUTHWEST................................Page   83

Chapter 4 — RAILS THROUGH THE ROCKIES..................Page 121

Chapter 5 — BY PACIFIC SHORES......................................Page 147

Chapter 6 — AN ALBUM OF WESTERN RAILROADS........Page 177

HIGH IN THE SNOW-CAPPED ROCKIES, a Colorado Midland passenger train stands on a spidery bridge near Buena Vista, Colorado, with cap-stacked 4-6-0 type Engine 17 heading the consist; the first car is a mail and baggage and the second an open-platform coach. The Colorado Midland Railroad ran through Hagerman Tunnel in the summit of the Continental Divide at Saguache Pass; the summit tunnel was located over 11,500 feet above sea level, giving the Midland claim to the highest standard gauge railroad pass in North America. The famed Midland "loop" leading to the original tunnel was difficult to keep open in winter, so the Busk Tunnel Railway Co. was formed in 1890 to bore a second tunnel through the Saguache Range at a lower altitude. This Busk-Ivanhoe tunnel was completed in 1893, was over three miles long, and the grades and curves leading to it were mild compared with the approach to the old Hagerman Tunnel. When the Colorado Midland was reorganized in 1897, the Busk Tunnel Company refused to allow the new operators to use the Busk-Ivanhoe tunnel, and the old Hagerman bore was cleared of its blockade of ice and the Midland trains ran over the original Midland Loop route for about 18 months before the hassle was settled and traffic reverted to the Busk tunnel line. When the United States Railroad Administration ordered the road abandoned, many of the Midland locomotives were shipped to France for use in World War I, and some came to Northwest logging lines.

(Wm. H. Jackson collection, courtesy of State Historical Society of Colorado)

MINNESOTA PIONEER, the famous old WM. CROOKS was the first locomotive to turn a wheel in the newly-formed state. The 4-4-0 was built by the New Jersey Locomotive & Machine Company at Paterson, N.J., and was delivered by rail to Prairie du Chien, Wisconsin. There she was loaded on a barge and towed up the Mississippi by the river steamboat, AL-HAMBRA. The locomotive and some cars and rail arrived at St. Paul on September 9, 1861, where the rail was unloaded at the levee at the foot of Sibley and Jackson streets; the engine and cars were landed near the mouth of Phalen Creek, one-half mile east, and placed in service between St. Paul and the village of St. Anthony, now Minneapolis. This photo was taken at Elk River, Minnesota, in 1864 and shows the WM. CROOKS in service on the 1st Div., St. Paul & Pacific Railroad. The engineer seated in the cab is Francis R. Delano, later Gen. Supt. of the road; standing is the fireman, James C. Morrison, later Purchasing Agent for the St. Paul, Minneapolis & Manitoba and afterward with the Great Northern's mechanical department. Delano, Minnesota, was named for the engineer shown here.

(Courtesy of Great Northern Railway)

Gateway to the Pacific.

Iron rails, laid in Minnesota by the St. Paul & Pacific Railroad in September of 1861, ushered rail-road transportation into the newly-formed state that was destined to be the springboard for the Northern Route transcontinental lines. The flow of commerce into the region was carried mainly by river steamers, resulting in irregular service depending on the condition of the waterways. Low water impeded the steamboats in the dry seasons and winter often sealed the navigable waters with a solid blockade of ice. The coming of the railroad was due to change all this, but even the early railroads within Minnesota's borders were dependent upon the river boats for the early years of their existence.

TWIN CITIES TERMINAL, this historic photograph taken in 1873 shows the Minneapolis station of the old St. Paul & Pacific Railroad. Directly behind the switch engine at left is the passenger station; the locomotive and two-car passenger train in the rear center stands at the left of the freight station. At far right, a funnel-stacked 4-4-0 heads a passenger train in front of a pioneer grain elevator. The freight house stood on the site of a later Great Northern Railway freight station located at Fourth Avenue, North, and the G.N. tracks. The grain elevator was among the first of a great many, the railroad bringing in a golden flow of grain from the western prairies to make Minneapolis one of the world's great grain storage and milling centers.
(Courtesy of Great Northern Railway)

ST. PAUL & PACIFIC RAILROAD acquired Engine 16 from the Danforth Locomotive & Machine Co. in 1869 and named her the KERKHOVEN, reflecting the influence of the Dutch bondholders who financed much of the early construction. The road was completed from St Paul to Breckenridge, Minnesota, on the Red River of the North, in 1871 and was in a receivership in 1873. The 4-4-0 KERKHOVEN joined sister engines bearing such names as EDMUND RICE, JUD RICE, ANOKA, JARED BENSON, F. R. DELANO, GEORGE L. BECKER, and WAYZATA. No. 16 had 63 inch drivers, 16 x 24 inch cylinders, and was a woodburner, later converted to coal. Under Great Northern control, she was renumbered 240 and scrapped in 1916.
(Courtesy of Great Northern Railway)

The first lines in Minnesota were purely local roads and it was not until 1867 that rail connections to the East were established. Even after that date, it was necessary to ferry equipment across the Mississippi for a number of years until the first bridges over the stream were constructed. Steamboats and barges moved locomotives, cars, and rails upstream to the embryo railway system, and the freight and passenger traffic collected by these local lines moved to the outside world via river boat.

The Twin Cities, St. Paul and St. Anthony, (the latter to become Minneapolis) held a key position to the great treasure chests of the northern plains region. Sharing in this control was Duluth, the shipping port at the western tip of Lake Superior.

With the westward expansion of the steel trails, an era of great development for all the Northwest began, and through these transportation strongholds flowed the rich stream of products and natural wealth. The railroad brought the sodbuster with his plow, the lumberman with his axe and sawmill, and the miner with his pick and shovel. Before their onslaught, the hills and prairies began to belch forth streams of traffic to roll to market over the frail iron of the pioneer railroads.

The pine forests of Minnesota and the neighboring state of Wisconsin proved a veritable Garden of Eden for the timber beasts who had slashed and hacked their way from the rocky hills of Maine. After denuding the Great Lakes region, they would later migrate to the pine of Idaho and the unbelievable firs and sequoias of the Pacific Coast. Pioneer logging was accomplished by driving the logs down the whitewater streams to the primitive sawmills, but when the forests were cut back from these watercourses, the lumbermen were quick to adapt the logging railroad to their method of operations. The ubiquitous Shay, with its slow speed, rapid exhaust, and powerful gear drive, made its reputation in the woods around the Great Lakes, spreading to wherever saws whined and timber toppled. Before Ephriam Shay perfected his iron mule, a variety of locomotives worked the logging pikes. At the start, most logging railroads were of flimsy construction, being intended for temporary "cut out and get out" use. Because of the light rail and frail bridges, small engines were the rule, many of them being worn-out kettles from regular rail lines.

As the demand for lumber increased, better roads were constructed to tap remote bodies of timber and many of these reached a high state of efficiency, with standards of roadbed and equipment measuring up favorably to common carrier roads. Indeed, some of them offered passenger service and even operated excursions. The interesting history of these big and little pikes can be found in an article, "Logging Railroads of Northern Minnesota," written by Franklin A. King and published in Bulletin 93 of the Railway & Locomotive Historical Society, Baker Library, Boston, Massachusetts.

The trail of the sod-buster led westerly, away from the timber claims where the Weyerhauesers and others were daylighting the swamps. Across the broad plains of Dakota Territory and into Montana stretched one of America's great grazing regions. Herds of buffalo so numerous as to defy counting had roamed these prairies before the coming of the white man, providing the native Indians with a roving commissary that supplied both food and shelter. The meat fed the tribesmen and the hides were used for building tepees, bull-boats, and other articles.

When the Army and the railroads vanquished the Indians, the buffalo was hunted to the point of extinction and the ranchers were quick to discover that cattle would thrive on the natural pasture that had sustained the shaggy herds of bison. Up the long trails from Texas and east from Oregon came the lowing cattle, stocking the ranges and establishing the livestock industry.

On the heels of the cattle rancher came the sheep man, and not far behind was the nester with his plow. This instrument murdered the buffalo grass, turning the endless sod into acres of grain fields. The cattle, sheep, and grain all meant business for the railroads, but the plowman turned much of the region into wasteland in later years. When the protective sod was removed, the sun and the wind eroded the exposed land, blowing away the rich top-soil and creating the American "Dust Bowl."

The Northern Pacific Railroad was the first to reach the upper waters of the Missouri, much of the surveying and ground work being carried out under protection of an Army escort. The rails, reaching from Duluth to Bismarck, invaded the tribal lands held sacred by the Sioux,

ST. PAUL & PACIFIC RAILROAD, pioneer Minnesota line, was justly proud of Engine 38, the G. W. TURNER. The 4-4-0 with the sunflower stack was outshopped by Rogers in August of 1878.   (Collection of Dr. S. R. Wood)

MEMORABLE DAY in the history of Devils Lake, North Dakota, was July 4th' 1883. The first train of the St. Paul, Minneapolis & Manitoba Railway rolled into town behind Engine 23, a trim three-domed American Standard. Flags, pennants, and evergreens decorated the engine and cars, and the townsfolk turned out to give the pioneer railroaders a hearty welcome. The uniform cap on the head of the conductor indicates that some of the niceties of Eastern operations have invaded the informal regions of the West. (Courtesy of Great Northern Railway)

and numerous brushes with the irate tribesmen livened up the advance of the survey groups.

New names were inked upon the maps, stations along the new track being named in honor of various railroad officers . . . Moorhead, Billings, Livingston. Financial problems caused reorganizations of the Company, yet the raw grade marched into the sunset and in 1883 the rails from Lake Superior met those from the Pacific Ocean at an isolated station in the Montana wilderness.

The web of tracks spread in all directions from the Twin Cities hub, south along the Mississippi, northwest to Manitoba, and west toward the former buffalo range. Up around Duluth, miners began extracting iron ore from Minnesota mines and the mineral wealth of the Mesabe Range came rolling down to the Duluth docks by rail.

This ore movement was seasonal, the winter freeze-up of the Great Lakes halting the ore boats and causing a lay-off of many railroaders. Herbert R. Rix was one of these enginemen who boomed around the West while cut off the working list due to the ore slump. A coal fireman, he drifted out to the West Coast and hired out on the Oregon Railway & Navigation Company; the engineer he was called to fire for had acquired a big steamboat whistle and every time

he blew this huge chime, the steam pressure in the small boiler of the eightwheeler would drop about 10 pounds. Rix had arrived in Portland expecting to hire out on the Southern Pacific. He hit town in the night and took a room in a hotel facing Fourth Street, where he was awakened early next morning by the sound of a locomotive laboring under his window. Leaping from his bed, he was amazed to see a diamond-stacker churning up the old West Side line through the heart of town, but the fuel in the tender was what staggered him. Two-foot sticks of splintery fir were piled up higher that the cab roof as the woodburner charged up the street, for the Espee continued to burn wood on the lines in Oregon until around 1910-12. The sight of this archaic "chip eater" caused him to seek employment of the O.R. & N., a coal road at the time, though he later gave up the Iron Range and served for many years as a fireman and engineer on the Espee's Portland Division.

The terrible winter of 1887 hit the railroads of Minnesota and the Dakotas with a fury that is still talked about by those old enough to remember. One man who vividly remembered this hard winter was Conductor E. S. Gunn, a veteran Chicago & North Western trainman. Gunn hired out on the North Western lines in Minnesota in 1884; a minor at the time, he had to obtain the traditional "release" signed by his father before he could go to work on the road. When the storms of 1887 began to pile up the snow, Gunn was working on the road and helped fight the battle to keep the line open. The North Western used snow-fighting technique that differed from the practice employed by roads in the Rockies and the Sierras. A single engine was fitted out with a pilot or "plunger" type of v-shaped snowplow and sent out to buck the deep drifts out of the cuts. A second locomotive, called the "drag-out" engine, followed the plow engine with a caboose, staying about a mile behind the snow buckers. When a drift was sighted, the engineer on the leading locomotive would widen on the throttle and head for the obstruction. Just before striking the drift the long-handled reverse lever was dropped down in the corner and the crew would brace themselves against the boiler head for the shock that was certain to follow. Gunn was braking on C&NW Engine 536 during the winter of '87, this engine being fitted out with a plow, and he recalled they would frequently be making 60 to 70 miles per hour when they hit a tough drift.

If the engine stayed on the rails and broke through the drift, all was well. If the plow stalled, however, the "drag-out" engine was whistled up and would couple into the stranded engine and pull it out of the drift for another attempt. This was dangerous work, but Gunn survived and served the Chicago & North Western for many years. When he retired in 1933 he was the conductor on the "Minnesota 400," running this passenger schedule between Winona and Mankato, Minnesota.

Other stories of winter railroading in Minnesota were handed down to the writer by his great-uncle, the late Adelmer Price. His first railroad job consisted of firing the water car on the snow train operating in western Minnesota. The sub-zero temperatures froze up most of the track-side water tanks and sometimes the engine of the snow train would be temporarily marooned in a drift until the section hands could dig it out. To prevent this locomotive from running out of water, a boxcar was fitted out with water tanks built inside, coupled to the regular tender tank of the engine with a hose. This car

WHEN JIM HILL MOVED WEST, his St. Paul, Minneapolis & Manitoba Railway used the terminal at Minot, North Dakota, as a jumping-off point. Track laying on the extension to the Pacific Coast was started at Minot on April 2, 1887, and 3,000 feet of rail was spiked home on the first day. About three miles west of Minot, the road crossed Gassman Coulee on the extensive wooden bridge shown here. Work on this structure was started in 1886 and the job was completed early in 1887. The span was 1,609 feet long, 102 feet high, and contained 1,303,998 feet of timber. On August 14, 1898, a wind storm blew down a portion of this wooden bridge and the Great Northern trains were routed around the break by means of a temporary shoo-fly a mile and one-half long that ran down into the coulee. While this detour was in use, the wooden bridge was replaced with a steel span 1,792 feet long and 117 feet high, the new structure being opened to traffic on January 6, 1899. Reinforced in the winter of 1923-24, it continues to serve the Great Northern well.
(Courtesy of Great Northern Railway)

Iron Horses Of The Northwest Gateway

ST. PAUL, MINNEAPOLIS & MANITOBA Engine 48 at Devil's Lake, North Dakota. The diamond stack 4-4-0 was built by Brooks and sports an entire deer head on her oil lamp instead of the customary set of antlers.
(Courtesy of Frek Jukes)

ROGERS LOCOMOTIVE WORKS turned out No 324 for the St. Paul, Minneapolis & Manitoba in 1887. The Mogul type was popular in that era, providing heavier power for freight service than the little 4-4-0 types of an earlier day.
(Collection of Dr. S. R. Wood)

also contained a large stove to prevent the water in the auxiliary tanks from freezing, and young Price was hired to stoke this heater. The duties were not too strenuous and he spent his spare time helping the train crew. Fascinated by the roaring road, this farm boy soon became so adept in switching that the crew put in a kindly word for him with the superintendent and Price was given a regular job as a brakeman. He later followed the rails west, serving as a brakeman on the Northern Pacific's switch-back over the Cascade Mountains in Washington. Returning to Minnesota, he was making up his train in the yards at Shakopee when he tripped on a pile of cinders left between the rails. His right hand, guiding the link into the drawhead slot, was crushed as he vainly attempted to regain his balance, ending his railroad service but never dimming his love of the iron road.

From the first humble beginnings around the Falls of St. Anthony, the railroads steadily expanded north and west, opening up the country and building the cities of the future. One by one, the short lines grew or were absorbed by larger systems to form a sprawling and efficient transportation machine. The logging pikes, such as the old "Gut and Liver," served their purpose and the crews migrated west, following the timber that receded before the onslaught of axe and saw. The crash of falling timber echoed in the Idaho pine and the fir of Oregon and Washington, and the pungent lumber rolled east over the northern transcontinentals, Northern Pacific, Great Northern, and Milwaukee Road.

The railroaders battled snow, dust, and grasshoppers, and came back for more. Braving the elements, they wheeled their puny trains across the broad prairies under a pall of acrid coal smoke, staining the blue bowl of sky that spread above the waving oceans of green grain. The Moguls and American Standards have faded away, but the same hardy breed of men still pilot the Diesel-powered drags and varnished cars where in yesteryear the crews cursed the Sand Coulee coal and juggled the link and pin.

The area surrounding the upper reaches of the Mississippi has long been termed the Gateway to the Northwest, and the railroads were the key that opened the lock to this colorful region.

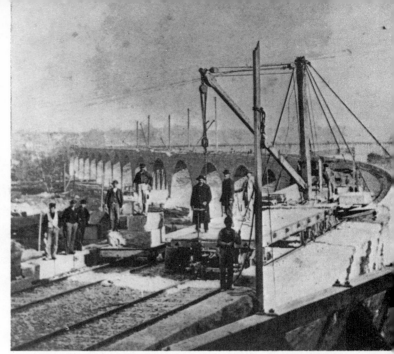

STONE ARCH BRIDGE over the Mississippi at Minneapolis was built in 1882-83 and cost $650,000. The 2,100 foot structure is still in use; the job took 18 months to complete.   (Courtesy of Great Northern Railway)

SWEEPING WEST ACROSS THE MONTANA PLAINS, the construction crews employed in building the St. Paul, Minneapolis & Manitoba were quartered in these huge dormitory cars. Much of the work on this Great Northern predecessor was done by the Grants, railroad construction contractors. This historic view shows Timekeeper John Grant seated in the buckboard; standing in the rear, left to right, are Contractor Donald Grant, Superintendent J. H. Benson, Paymaster Cox, and the unidentified camp doctor, holding his traditional bag of equipment. At the doctor's left stands an Indian visitor, come to inspect the advance of the Iron Horse. This photo, taken in 1887, shows a buffalo skull and a set of deer antlers mounted on the dormitory car in the foreground; a rain or a thaw has softened the grade, and gumbo clings to the wheels of the horse-drawn rigs. These over-sized bunk cars served well on the open plains of the Dakota and Montana sections of the road, but when the mountains were reached, the limitations of the tunnels made it necessary to saw them off to standard heights of clearance.   (Courtesy of Great Northern Railway)

"WHEN OUR GANG CAME OUT FROM SUPPER" was the original caption affixed to this photo taken in Montana Territory in 1887. The crew engaged in building the St. Paul, Minneapolis & Manitoba west from Minot, Dakota Territory, to Helena was probably the Grant Brothers' construction outfit. Interested spectators in the group of whiskery railroad builders included a number of visiting Indians, visible here in the foreground. Although several of them have adopted various items of the white man's dress, these natives still wear their hair long and a number of them are swathed in the traditional

blanket. The hatless railroader standing at left in the front rank holds a papoose, apparently naked except for a head cloth. Amicable relations were maintained with the tribesmen and the cookhouse helped cement these friendly feelings with hand-outs from the contractors' mess supplies. Fresh in the minds of red men and white alike were the bitter memories of a decade previous, when rifle and tomahawk drenched the plains with the blood of both races, but these dark recollections were buried as the iron trails were driven toward the setting sun.   (Courtesy of Great Northern Railway)

FLINT & PERE MARQUETTE RAILWAY was a Michigan pike organized in 1857 and, after absorbing several short lines, was opened for service in 1874 between Monroe and Luddington. Engine 3 was built by Schenectady in 1871, bearing Shop No. 695.

(Collection of Dr. S. R. Wood)

PATRIOTIC PRIDE is reflected in this decorated American Standard, resplendent with polish, flags, rosettes, bunting, and evergreens. The engine is the Great Northern's No. 207, and the occasion was a 4th of July celebration in the 1890's, the photo being taken at Barnesville or Crookston, Minnesota. The 4-4-0 was built by Rogers at Paterson, New Jersey, in 1887. Note the side-door caboose, or way car, No. 09, in the left background. The term, way car, was seldom applied to cabooses on lines along the Pacific Coast, the expression there referring to the car for local or way freight which was customarily kept on the head end of freight trains.

(Courtesy of Great Northern Railway)

TYPICAL LOGGING ENGINE used around the Great Lakes was No. 2 of the narrow gauge Mason & Oceana Railroad, running out of Buttersville, Michigan. She bore Lima's Shop No. 154 and was built in 1886. (Collection of Dr. S. R. Wood)

GREAT NORTHERN RAILWAY's No. 658 is shown here at Devil's Lake, North Dakota, in the 1890's, backed by the frame depot and one of the towering grain elevators that rose like monuments along the "Big G" lines through the grain belt. The fireman seated in the cab is the late Alvanley Johnson, who for many years held the helm of the Brotherhood of Locomotive Engineers; as he takes a brief respite here from his labors with scoop, he perhaps little dreams that some day he will be elevated to the position of Grand Chief Engineer of that old and honored railroad labor organization. The big 4-6-0 with the Belpaire boiler was built by the Brooks Locomotive Works in 1893; she had 19 x 26 inch cylinders and 73 inch drivers, suited for fast stepping with the varnished cars across the Dakota plains. A sister engine of the locomotive shown here, Great Northern's No. 650, was exhibited at the Chicago World's Fair in 1893, along with a number of other locomotives representing the acme of railroad motive power in use at the time. Devil's Lake, located in North Dakota's Ramsey County, is on the G.N. main line from Crookston west to the Pacific, and in the heart of the "picket fence" region, a district so named because the numerous Great Northern branch lines running toward the Canadian line appear on maps in such profusion as to resemble a picket fence.   (Courtesy of Fred Jukes)

MINNESOTA VALLEY RAILROAD, one of the pioneer lines in Minnesota, was absorbed by the St. Paul & Sioux City Railroad, later becoming a part of the present Chicago, St. Paul, Minneapolis & Omaha Railway. By November of 1870 the St. Paul & Sioux City had opened 121 miles of track from St. Paul to St. James, Minnesota, where the line connected with the Sioux City & St. Paul Railroad; the Sioux City & St. Paul was completed in 1872, running from St. James, Minnesota, to Le Mars, Iowa, where it operated over the Iowa Division of the Illinois Central for 26 miles into the Sioux City terminus. The unusual piece of equipment pictured is the Minnesota Valley road's SHAKOPEE, a combination locomotive and coach with a baggage compartment. The single-drivered engine was built in the shops of the Columbus & Indianapolis Railway in Columbus, Ohio, about 1865 by Master Mechanic W. Romans. Accompanied by James Drugan, the SHAKOPEE was taken by rail to La Crosse, Wisconsin, then barged up to Mendota, northern terminus of the Minnesota Valley road, where Mechanic Drugan put it in running order. Other locomotives on the road included the MANKATO, ST. PETER, and BELLE PLAINE. (Courtesy of Charles E. Fisher)

WEST WISCONSIN RAILWAY was chartered in April, 1863, and on December 1, 8712, opened for service 177 miles of standard gauge line from Hudson to Elroy, Wisconsin. The road connected with the Chicago & North Western Railway at Elroy and leased rights over the Stillwater & St. Paul Railroad on the western end, thus forming a direct connection between St. Paul and Chicago. The 42 miles of the North Wisconsin Railroad from Hudson Junction to Clayton, Wisconsin, were operated by the West Wisconsin Railway, and the Chippewa Falls & Western Railroad was also operated as a leased line. The latter pike, opened in 1874, extended 11 miles from Eau Claire to Chippewa Falls. This interesting old photo was taken at the West Wisconsin Ry. roundhouse at Eau Claire in 1871. The workmen in the foreground are framing a new wooden turntable; the locomotives in the rear are all Baldwin woodburners of the 4-4-0 type, built in 1871. Headed out of Stall 7 at left is No. 12, the GEO. W. CLINTON; the engine headed into Stall 6, with her tender missing and main rods down, is No. 14, the MATT H. CARPENTER; backed into Stall 3 is No. 10, the D. A. BALDWIN; at far right, Stall 1, stands No. 11, the T. HUMBERT. In the lower right foreground, between the old "armstrong" turntable and the wooden base for the new turntable, stands a "butterfly" or pilot snowplow, ready to be bolted to the front of a locomotive when winter's snow blanketed the Wisconsin woodlands. The locomotives pictured here all carried their same numbers on the Chicago, St. Paul, Milwaukee & Omaha when that road took over the West Wisconsin. (Collection of Dr. S. R. Wood)

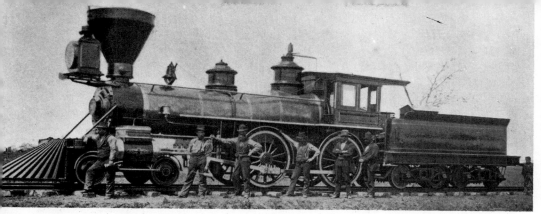

PEMBINA BRANCH OF CANADIAN PACIFIC was built by Contractor Joseph Whitehead, a former locomotive fireman and engineer from the Stockton & Darlington Railway in England; he had been present when that historic line was first opened in 1825. Grading on the Manitoba road started in July, 1877, and a connection was made with the St. Paul, Minneapolis & Manitoba Railroad at Emerson, on the Manitoba-Minnesota border. The first through passenger train ran on December 2nd, 1877, and the first through freight train from eastern Canada rolled over the line to St. Boniface on December 23rd, the cars being routed via Chicago and St. Paul. Engine No. 2 on the Pembina road was a 4-4-0 named the JOSEPH WHITEHEAD, but nicknamed the STAR, after the emblem on her smokebox plate. A Baldwin product of 1878, she bore Shop No. 4319, had 17 x 24 inch cylinders and 60 inch drivers. In 1882 she became Canadian Pacific Railway's No. 144 and was scrapped in 1902. John Parkington was her first engineer and Stephen Parkington her first fireman. Other Whitehead contract engines included the JAMES McKAY, JAMES M. ROWAN, EMPRESS OF INDIA, SITTING BULL, and JOSEPH BROPHY. Mr. W. H. Swinbank, fireman on No. 3, the JAMES McKAY, was a great grandson of George Stephenson; he later fired the first regular passenger west of Winnipeg for Engineer Ash Kennedy, consisting of 13 coaches hauled by Canadian Pacific's Engine No. 60. (Courtesy of Canadian Pacific Railway)

HISTORIC SHIPMENT OF RAIL EQUIPMENT is shown in this rare photograph taken on October 9th, 1877. On that day, the sternwheeler SELKIRK churned up the Red River of the North to the Winnipeg landing with a barge loaded with rolling stock for the projected Pembina Branch of the infant Canadian Pacific. This shipment was unloaded at St. Boniface, across the river from Winnipeg, and placed in service on the Pembina Branch; although lettered "Canadian Pacific," it was actually owned by Joseph Whitehead, the contractor engaged in building the line from the Manitoba metropolis south to the American Boundary. The cargo consisted of six flat cars, a caboose or "van," and Engine No. 1, the COUNTESS OF DUFFERIN. The locomotive was a 4-4-0 built by Baldwin in 1872, Shop No. 2660. She had 15 x 24 inch cylinders, 57 inch drivers, and was purchased by Whitehead from the Northern Pacific in 1877 for $6,800. Previously numbered Northern Pacific 56, she was given No. 1 by Whitehead, and when the Pembina line was acquired by the Canadian Pacific in 1881-82. she became C.P.R. No. 151. In 1897 she was sold to the Columbia River Lumber Co. at Golden, British Columbia, but was returned to Winnipeg in 1910 and is preserved there as a relic on public display. Her first crew on the Pembina Branch consisted of Engr. J. Cardell and Fireman G. C. Swinbank. (Courtesy of Canadian Pacific Railway)

CANADIAN PACIFIC RAILWAY station at Portage la Prairie, Manitoba, forms the backdrop for this view of the CPR's No. 92 and her three passenger cars in 1892. The 4-4-0 was built in the United States by Rhode Island Locomotive Works in 1882, had 69 inch drivers and 17 x 24 inch cylinders.

A HEAVY DRAG, consisting of 12 coaches and 2 box cars, are tied on behind Canadian Pacific's No. 129, a diamond stack 4-4-0 built by Rhode Island in 1883. The big consist on the level prairie line was either an excursion or an immigrant train of settlers examining the broad plains for farmsites. Engine 129, a hand-fired coalburner, had 17 x 24 inch cylinders and 62 inch drivers, and was one of a series of 11 locomotives built by the American firm for the Canadian road; numbered 120 to 130 by the CPR, they bore Shop No's. 1339 to 1349. (Both photos, courtesy of Canadian Pacific Railway)

DULUTH, SOUTH SHORE & ATLANTIC RAILWAY, controlled by the Canadian Pacific, was formed late in 1886 by the consolidation of a number of older roads, including the Sault Ste. Marie & Marquette Railroad, Duluth, Superior & Michigan Railway, Mackinaw & Marquette Railroad, and the Wisconsin, Sault Ste. Marie & Mackinaw Railway. The main stem extended along the southern reaches of Lake Superior from Sault Ste. Marie, Michigan, to West Superior, Wisconsin, 408 miles, with branches tapping the mining and timber regions. Engine 4, upper, was an old 0-4-0 built by New Jersey Locomotive Works in 1862. Engine 404, lower, was a 2-6-0 built by Baldwin in 1884, Shop No. 7189; she was constructed as No. 54 for the Marquette & Ishpeming Construction Company.

(Both photos, collection of Dr. S. R. Wood)

MINNEAPOLIS, ST. PAUL & SAULT STE. MARIE RAILWAY was formed in June, 1888, by a consolidation of the Minneapolis & St. Croix Ry., Minneapolis, Sault Ste. Marie & Atlantic Ry., Minneapolis & Pacific Ry., and the Aberdeen, Bismarck & Northwestern Railway. The main stem extended 1,038 miles from Sault Ste. Marie, Michigan, to Portal, North Dakota, where a connection with the controlling Canadian Pacific carried the road into Moose Jaw, Saskatchewan. Branch lines served numerous locations in Michigan, Wisconsin, Minnesota, and the Dakotas, including the "Wheat Line" from Thief River Falls, Minnesota, to Kenmare, North Dakota. The Soo Line now has expanded to a system containing over 4,000 miles of track, with executive headquarters established in Minneapolis. The diamond stack 4-4-0 shown here is the Soo Line's No. 42, a Baldwin product of 1886. She was erected under Baldwin construction number 8197; a sister engine was Soo Line 303, another Baldwin 4-4-0 built in 1886 as No. 14 of the Minneapolis & Pacific.

(Collection of Dr. S. R. Wood)

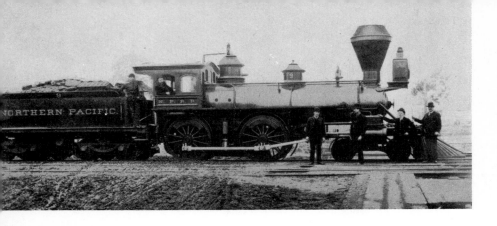

EARLY N. P. STANDARD, this coal-burning 4-4-0 was built for the road by Baldwin in July, 1871, and became Northern Pacific's No. 9. She rolled out of the Philadelphia works with Shop No. 2490 on her builders' plates and was placed in service on the eastern end of the road. When the Northern Pacific tracks were extended toward the Pacific, a fleet of similar 4-4-0's were acquired to handle the additional traffic; these included locomotives built by Baldwin, the Portland Locomotive Works of Portland, Maine, and the New York Locomotive Works of Rome, New York.

(Courtesy of Dr. S. R. Wood)

LAKE SUPERIOR & MISSISSIPPI RAILROAD was chartered on May 23, 1857, but actual operations did not start until September, 1868. The road built north from St. Paul, Minnesota, and by early 1870 the line was operating 75 miles of standard gauge trackage to Hinckley. The line between St. Paul and Duluth, 156 miles, was opened for through service on August 1, 1870; in common with other pioneer Minnesota roads, the early engines and rolling stock were brought up the Mississippi by river steamboats. On June 20, 1868, the steamer FAVORITE delivered a locomotive at St. Paul for the Lake Superior & Mississippi which was reportedly the first Baldwin engine to arrive in Minnesota; weighing 31 tons, this locomotive had 16 x 24 inch cylinders and was named the WILLIAM L. BANNING, after the president of the line. The road also leased and operated the Stillwater & St. Paul Railroad, a 13 mile pike running from Stillwater to White Bear. The Lake Superior & Mississippi later was reorganized as the St. Paul & Duluth Railway, known as the "Skally Line," and is now a part of the Northern Pacific Railway. This rare view of 1871 shows Lake Superior & Mississippi Engine 6, a wood-burning 0-6-0, at the freight depot along the Duluth waterfront, near the present 3rd Avenue East.

(Courtesy of Northern Pacific Railway)

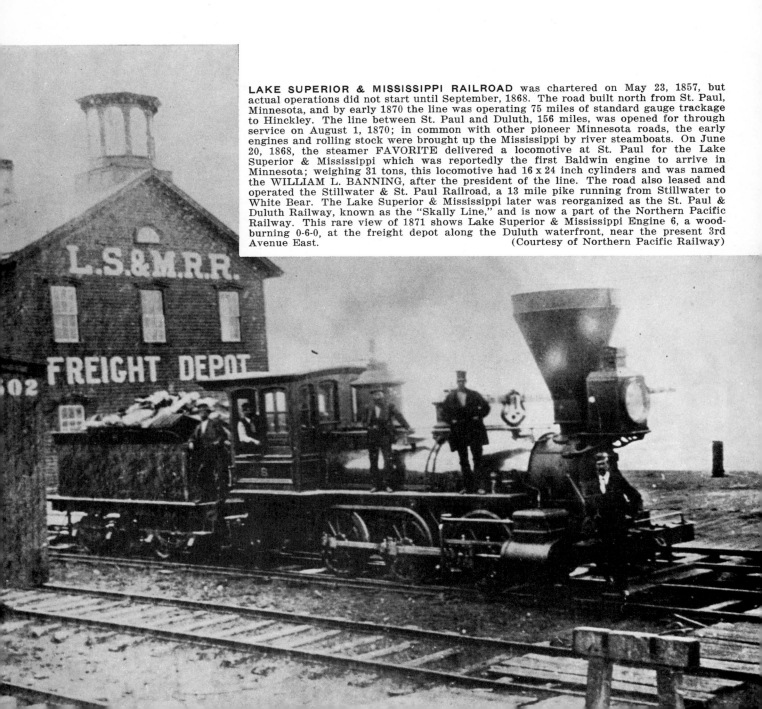

HENRY VILLARD's "BLIND POOL" was formed early in 1881 to provide the financial ammunition for his battle to gain control of the Northern Pacific, and in the same year the Baldwin Locomotive Works turned out a Mogul bearing Shop No. 5566. This engine became Northern Pacific's No. 79, a 2-6-0 designed for heavy freight duty. She served faithfully until outmoded, then was converted into an 0-6-0 for yard service and renumbered 949. This photo shows the engine as originally built when she was wheeling drags over the road that was later to lay claim to the title of "The Main Street of the Northwest."

(Courtesy of Dr. S. R. Wood)

ST. PAUL & DULUTH RAILROAD was the successor of the old Lake Superior & Mississippi Railroad, extending from Duluth to St. Paul, Minnesota. This photo shows Engine No. 2 with a passenger train at Pine City, Minnesota, in 1883; note the logs strewn along the track in the foreground. Thirteen miles north of Pine City was Hinckley, a mill town destroyed in the terrible forest fire that ravaged eastern Minnesota in September, 1894. Heroes of the Hinckley fire included several St. Paul & Duluth railroaders. Engineer James Root and Fireman Jack McGowan, the crew on southbound Train No 4, the "Duluth Limited," met the refugees from Hinckley streaming up the tracks, flames licking at their heels. These fugitives from the red demon were loaded aboard and the train backed up to Skunk Lake, a shallow swamp some six miles to the north. Engineer Root, a veteran who had run an engine for Sherman in Georgia, stuck to his post until the place of safety was reached, although badly burned. Fireman McGowan doused the engineer with pails of water to enable him to complete his mercy run. John Blair, a colored porter, also played a hero's role, calming the passengers and dousing the fires that the intense heat ignited inside the cars. The train was destroyed, but the lives of those aboard were saved by the bravery of the train and engine crew.

(Courtesy of Northern Pacific Railway)

NORTHERN PACIFIC'S No. 216 was a pretty 4-4-0 built by the Portland Locomotive Works in 1882, bearing Shop No. 423. The simple lines of her straight boiler are graced by the ornately-scrolled headlight bracket and her clean rods and jacket are indicative of good care on the part of her crew and the mechanical department. This woodburner later became Northern Pacific's No. 893.   (Courtesy of Dr. S. R. Wood)

WINTER ON THE NORTHERN PLAINS brought forth the assembled efforts of railroaders to keep the tracks clear and the trains operating. Pictured here are two Northern Pacific locomotives bucking the drifts with a pilot plow after a heavy snowfall. Note that the headlights of both engines have been covered to protect the lens, and that the front and side cab windows of the leading locomotive are protected by wooden slats. The steam hose coiled around the sand dome of the Portland-built 4-4-0 in the lead was used for thawing frozen snow out of the link blocks of her valve gear; the canvas draped over her tender sheltered the fuel supply from snow tossed high in the air by the plow.

(Courtesy of Dr. S. R. Wood)

A LONG WAY FROM DIXIE! This historic photograph shows a 4-4-0 of the Northern Pacific hauling a train over track laid on the frozen surface of the Missouri River between Bismarck and Mandan, Dakota Territory, in the severe winter of 1878-79. In the summer months, the trains were ferried across the Missouri until the completion of the railroad bridge. The gentleman wearing the cape in the center foreground is General Thomas L. Rosser, a former General in the Confederate Army and a Northern Pacific construction engineer in Dakota Territory at the time this photo was taken.
(Northern Pacific photo, courtesy of Association of American Railroads)

TRAINS OF THE NORTHERN PACIFIC were ferried across the Missouri River between Bismarck and Mandan, Dakota Territory, prior to the completion of the railroad bridge at that point. This historic view shows Northern Pacific Engine 51, an 0-4-0 Baldwin, dragging a string of freight cars off the deck of the big sidewheeler used as a transfer boat in the summer of 1879. Note the crude ferry slip, with the hewn ties laid on a cribbing of timbers out to the point where the shallow draft steamer was able to nose up to a set of piling dolphins. When the winter freeze-up put an end to the car ferrying, the tracks were laid across the frozen surface of the Missouri, as shown in another photograph in this book.
(Northern Pacific photo, courtesy of Association of American Railroads)

WILL IT HOLD? A crowd of interested spectators gaze in wonder as the Northern Pacific Railroad tests the big bridge across the Missouri River near Mandan, North Dakota, in 1880. Eight diamond-stacked 4-4-0 type locomotives were coupled up and operated across the lengthy spans and adjoining trestle work to test the strength of the structures. This bridge on the main line of the northern transcontinental route ended the Northern Pacific's summer train ferry and winter "ice bridge" across the waters of the Big Muddy. The towering stone piers supported the metal truss spans, the wooden false-work visible here under the spans being removed as soon as the work was completed. Although the bridge was designed by competent and skilled artisans, one cannot but wonder at the thoughts of the enginemen in charge of this battery of motive power as they chuffed out onto the structure for the trial trip across it. The gifted railroad author, Frank H. Spearman, in his book, "The Strategy of Great Railroads," remarked, "Western railroad men are in themselves a tower of strength. They stand for decision, action, and organization. They are indefatigable, constructive, and, above all, resourceful . . ." Spearman's statements hold true to this day, but incidents such as this bridge trial at the risk of life and limb are, happily, no longer a common occurrence. (Courtesy of Ronald V. Nixon)

BEVY OF BALLOON STACKERS line up for the photographer at the Northern Pacific's brick roundhouse located in Billings Montana, in this view taken in 1884. The "gallows" style wooden turntable in the foreground is typical of the equipment in use at that time for turning locomotive; at the right side in the immediate foreground can be seen the wooden arm or handle, against which the men pushed in order to furnish the necessary power to revolve the turntable. These manually-operated affairs were known as "Arm-strong" or "Strong Arm" types, and many roads continued to use them for lighter power on branch line facilities until modern times; the writer has helped turn Diesel locomotives on hand-powered turntables similar to the one shown here. Note the huge headlight or pilot snowplow on the engine standing in the stall at far left. (Courtesy of Ronald V. Nixon)

BALDWIN'S 10,000th LOCOMOTIVE was a Consolidation type turned out in May, 1889. The cap-stacked 2-8-0 had 22 x 28 inch cylinders and 50 inch driving wheels. She was sold to the Northern Pacific, where she was assigned road number 10000; later she was renumbered N P. 460, then 98, and ended her days as No. 55. This photo shows her as originally constructed with link and pin coupler, spoked engine wheels in her leading truck, and a wooden cab with the name, BALDWIN, inscribed under the engineer's arm rest in the center cab window. (Courtesy of Association of American Railroads)

SHERMAN HOUSE, historic old frontier hostelry located in Bismarck, North Dakota, also served as the Northern Pacific depot when that road was building west. This view of the big wooden frame structure, showing its porticoed gallery and railed balconies, was taken in 1880, about the time the nearby railroad bridge across the Missouri was completed. The diamond stacked American Standard posed in front of the hotel is the Northern Pacific's No. 37, a typical road engine of the day. Although isolated in the wilds of the frontier, the railroaders building the Northern Pacific did not forget the amenities of civilization and institutions such as the Sherman House provided the comforts so often found lacking in the Far West. The commissary department of the Northern Pacific provided the construction engineers with a remarkably varied cuisine, prepared by the best cooks obtainable, for railroad crews, like armies, travel on their stomachs. When Engineer J. B. Clough's headquarters celebrated Thanksgiving in Miles City, Montana, in 1881, the menu included a wide variety of delicacies and staples. Guests were offered oysters, trout, salmon, turkey, chicken, venison, mountain sheep, elk, loin of buffalo, and the commonplace beef and mutton, in addition to a choice selection of fruits, vegetables, and desserts. Liquid refreshments were also available along the line, and frontier Billings sported three saloons named Blue Grass, Bunch Grass, and Buffalo Grass. (Courtesy of Ronald V. Nixon)

FUNERAL SPECIAL was photographed on the Northern Pacific's Mott Branch about 1910, bearing the body of an Indian woman to her final resting place. The tribesmen are escorting the remains from N.P. Extra 530 to the horsedrawn rigs waiting in the ravine at the left, ready to leave for the burial site overlooking the wide Missouri. The Indians were residents of the Standing Rock Indian Reservation; the Mott Branch was built south from Mandan, North Dakota, through Fort Rice to Cannon Ball Junction, thence west through Fisher and New Leipzig to Mott. In 1881, the Army moved over 1,600 Sioux of various tribes from Fort Keogh, Montana, to the Standing Rock Reservation, the tribesmen being the remnants of the hostiles that had defeated Custer and waged a bitter campaign to retain their hunting grounds. The mass exodus was made by five Missouri River steamboats, the vessels including the GENERAL TERRY, the JOSEPHINE, and the ECLIPSE, the latter being the flagship under command of Capt. Grant Marsh, famous Missouri River steamboat skipper. It was Capt. Marsh who piloted the FAR WEST to the mouth of the Little Big Horn to bring out the wounded from the Custer battlefield in 1876. In 1873, the river steamboats FAR WEST, KEY WEST, JOSEPHINE, and PENINAH were used by General Stanley to supply troops guarding the Northern Pacific surveyors working near the mouth of Glendive Creek.

(Courtesy of Ronald V. Nixon)

CONFUSION OF ORDERS sent these two Northern Pacific trains into a head-on collision on the windswept barrens of western North Dakota in 1905. The two passenger trains involved were both being doubleheaded, Train 4 being handled by Engines 241 and 249 and Train 5 wheeling along behind Engines 240 and 2127. The train orders in use at the time were handwritten, and one of the flimsies gave the two strings of varnish at straight meet at Knowlton. Due to a similarity in names, the crew of one train mis-read the operator's scrawled "Knowlton" for "Richardton," another station nearby. The results of this mistake are graphically depicted in this photo, showing the four locomotives locked together on the snowy plains. To prevent a recurrence of this accident, Knowlton station was immediately renamed Boyle. This is but one of many such instances found in the annals of Western railroading, and the wonder is that such lapses were not more frequent; one Western line, in its early days, had stations named Riverview, Riverside, and Riverdale, all located in close proximity. The use of the typewriter for transcribing train orders also was a help in eliminating such mistakes, proving far more legible than many specimens of the old "op fist" of scrawled and looped words written by hand with stylus and carbon on the thin tissue used for train orders. Note the heavy coating of frost on the head-end cars at right in this photo, silent testimony to the bitter cold that chilled the plains in winter.

(Courtesy of Ronald V. Nixon)

REAR-END COLLISION on the Northern Pacific near Fertile, Minnesota, took place about the turn of the century. This photo shows the freakish effects of the crash; the force of the impact of collision has driven the caboose neatly on top of a flat car, while a second flat car has knocked out the entire front end of the caboose and passed more than half of its length inside the crummy, leaving the caboose walls and roof practically intact. The locomotive involved in this rear-ender is nearly buried beneath the wooden box cars that have hurtled to rest upon it. Fertile is located in northwestern Minnesota, on the line from Manitoba Junction to Winnipeg, Canada, via Crookston, Grand Forks, and Pembina. No details have come down regarding this accident, but such happenings were all too frequent in earlier times. Rear end collisions had a wide variety of causes; trains following too close before the advent of block signals; improper flagging; trains running out of control down grades and unable to stop, and other reasons. Before the air brake came into general use, trains could not be stopped in time when the rear man gave a short flag or when fog and snow obliterated the signals and reduced visibility; before the 16 Hour Law was passed, sleepy enginemen dozed off and ran by the flagman, often paying the supreme price for a few moments of "shut-eye" brought on by long, grueling hours on duty.　　　　　　　　(Courtesy of Ronald V. Nixon)

HECLA & TORCH LAKE RAILROAD was built in 1868 to serve the copper mines of Michigan. The short line, 7.5 miles long, linked Hecla with Calumet and Lake Linden, and was built to the unusual gauge of 4 feet, 1 inch. In its glory days the road operated 14 locomotives; the KITCHIGAMI, shown here, was a 2-8-0 built by Baldwin in 1885, Shop No. 7709. This locomotive sported a Mother Hubbard style cab and a wide Wooten firebox, carried above the frames to allow more grate area; the roof over the gangway and front of the tender sheltered the fireboy as he bailed in the black diamonds. After many years of moving vast mountains of copper ore, the Hecla & Torch Lake was abandoned in 1908.

(Collection of Dr. S. R. Wood)

MILWAUKEE & WAUKESHA RAILROAD, chartered in 1847, was the parent road of the present Chicago, Milwaukee, St. Paul & Pacific. Renamed Milwaukee & Mississippi Railroad in 1850, the road was completed from Milwaukee to Milton, Wisconsin, late in 1851; a junction with the Southern Wisconsin Railroad, later absorbed into the system, carried the rails on to Janesville. The Madison & Prairie du Chien Railroad, started in 1852, was consolidated with the Milwaukee & Waukesha in 1853; this line was completed from Milwaukee to Madison, 105 miles, by December of 1854 and the westward extension reached the Mississippi at Prairie du Chien in 1857. The northern route from Milwaukee was formed by the consolidation of several roads, including the La Crosse & Milwaukee, the Milwaukee, Fond du Lac & Green Bay, and the Milwaukee & Watertown, reaching the Mississippi at La Crosse in 1858. The Milwaukee & St. Paul Railroad, organized in 1863, absorbed the lines above, and in 1867 gave Minnesota the first rail link with the East. The Minnesota Central had built a road from the Twin Cities south to Owatonna, Minnesota, and the McGregor Western Railway had built from North McGregor, Iowa, to Cresco, 62 miles. The Milwaukee & St. Paul purchased these roads and built 82 miles to connect them. Ferry service carried the trains over the Mississippi, the Prairie du Chien & McGregor Railway completing a bridge between those points in 1874; this bridge, using two pontoon draws, was used by the M&StP on a toll basis. M&StP Engine 37, the FRED MERRILL, was built by Norris in 1848 for the Milwaukee & Waukesha. (Collection of Dr. S. R. Wood)

MILWAUKEE & ST. PAUL RAILROAD was renamed the Chicago, Milwaukee & St. Paul Railway early in 1874. The original road acquired the St. Paul & Chicago Railroad, running up the west bank of the Mississippi from La Crescent, opposite La Crosse, in 1872, the year it was completed. Later acquisitions included such historic Minnesota roads as the Southern Minnesota Railroad and the Hastings & Dakota Railroad, along with the Minnesota Central Railroad. The Hastings & Dakota line ran from Hastings, on the Mississippi, to Glencoe, crossing the north-south route of the Minnesota Central at Farmington. The Southern Minnesota Railroad operated from Grand Crossing, opposite La Crosse, but the initial construction started around Hokah, on the Root River some 8 miles west of its junction with the Mississippi. The first engine, shipped up the Root River to Hokah, bore the name SHERWOOD in honor of a director, Lieutenant Governor Sherwood. This road formed the eastern end of the present Milwaukee line running west to Albert Lea, Mankato, and Pipestone. When the road was completed from Hokah to the Mississippi, the river was solidly frozen over and the first shipments of freight were hauled across on the ice by teams to the La Crosse connection. Part of the Milwaukee lines in Iowa were acquired through the purchase of the Sabula, Ackley & Dakota Railroad, 87 miles from Sabula to Marion. Engine 222 of the Chicago Milwaukee & St. Paul is shown here at Madrid, Iowa, in 1890. Schenectady's No. 1093, the neat 4-4-0 was built in August, 1878. (Collection of Dr. S. R. Wood)

GENERAL GRANT WAS HERE. Engine No. 209 of the Chicago, Milwaukee & St Paul Railway was built by Schenectady in September, 1877, bearing Shop No. 1065. In April of 1899 the diamond stacked 4-4-0 was renumbered 750, and in 1912 she was renumbered 203. Her claim to fame was made on June 9th, 1880, when she was marked up to haul the special train bearing General Ulysses Simpson Grant from Chicago to Milwaukee. Grant, noted Civil War commander and President of the United States from 1869 until 1877, was bound for Milwaukee to attend the Annual Encampment of the Grand Army of the Republic, an association of Union veterans of the War Between the States. The Chicago, Milwaukee & St. Paul Railway, forerunner of the present Chicago, Milwaukee, St. Paul & Pacific Railroad, polished up Engine 209 for the occasion and the high-stepping American Standard whisked the General from Chicago to Milwaukee in 2 hours 10 minutes running time. Average time for modern passenger trains between the two cities is about 1 hour 40 minutes, with heavy rail and the best of present-day motive power.

(Chicago, Milwaukee, St. Paul & Pacific photo, courtesy of Association of American Railroads)

CHICAGO & PACIFIC RAILWAY started life as the Atlantic & Pacific Railroad, a line projected from Chicago to the Mississippi River and having no relationship with the later Atlantic & Pacific road that formed a part of the Santa Fe's route across the Southwest. Chartered on February 16, 1865, the Atlantic & Pacific Railroad was reorganized as the Chicago & Pacific Railway on April 30, 1872. By 1874 the road had 88 miles of track in operation between Chicago and Byron, Illinois. Financial problems brought about a foreclosure sale in 1879, the line being purchased by the Chicago, Milwaukee & St. Paul. Engine No. 2 of the Chicago & Pacific was built by Rogers, Shop No. 2191, in 1873. As the plate on her jacket indicates, she was named the T. S. DOBBINS, being named in honor of Thomas S. Dobbins of Chicago, president of the road. Note the fancy woodwork applied around her cab windows and panels and the exceptional length of her diamond stack. Poor's Railroad Manual of the United States lists 5 locomotives on the Chicago & Pacific roster at the close of 1876.

(Collection of Dr. S. R. Wood)

RAILROAD HISTORIANS often credit the Baldwin Locomotive Works with the initial construction of the 4-6-2, or Pacific, type of locomotives, thirteen lignite-burning engines of this wheel arrangement having been built for export to the New Zealand Government Railways in 1901. However, the Chicago, Milwaukee & St. Paul had a locomotive with this wheel arrangement in service around 1890. Engine 796 was built for the Milwaukee by Schenectady in 1889, Shop No. 2855. The engine was designed as a 4-6-0- but was found to carry too much weight on her drivers and a trailing set of wheels was added, making her a 4-6-2 type. In April, 1899, the engine had her road number changed to 191, and in November, 1903, she was renumbered 850. In October, 1912, the Pacific type was rebuilt to a conventional 4-6-0 and given road number 6000, later being renumbered 2185 in January, 1926. This photo shows the husky coalburner as she appeared when equipped with the trailing truck that made her an authentic 4-6-2 type. (Collection of Dr. S. R. Wood)

MILWAUKEE ROAD TRAINS came to an unscheduled meeting point in the shady woodlands near Coaldale, Iowa, in 1903. The road where the head-on collision took place was the Chicago, Milwaukee & St. Paul's line running between Des Moines and Spirit Lake. Engine 49, at left, was originally No. 466, a 4-6-0 built by Rhode Island in October, 1881, Shop No. 1053. She later became No. 2058 and was cut up in 1926. The pair of ten-wheelers on the double-header at right are not identified. The bright sunlight, shirt-sleeved spectators, and the straw skimmer on the gent at left all indicate a warm day, and the chances are better than good that some of the bottled beer piled near the "bob-wire" fence in the foreground will evaporate before the sweating members of the wrecking crew get this mess cleaned up. (Collection of Dr. S. R. Wood)

CROWD OF CURIOUS SPECTATORS gathered at Mitchell, South Dakota, to view the results of this head-on collision between Engines 623 and 659 of the Chicago, Milwaukee & St. Paul Railway. Engineer Sumner and Fireman Weiland were killed in this bad smash which occurred on October 7, 1907. Engine 623 was Rhode Island's Shop No. 971, built in May of 1881 as the 447; she was renumbered 623 in 1899, became the 323 in 1912 and was scrapped in 1926. Engine 659 was also a Rhode Island product, constructed in February, 1882, under Shop No. 1138. Originally bearing road number 552, she acquired number 659 in the general renumbering of April, 1899. Later she was renumbered 359 in 1912 and was scrapped in 1920. Although the engines do not appear to have incurred serious damage in the wreck shown here, the cabs of both locomotives are practically demolished. Mitchell, South Dakota, played an important role in the Milwaukee's operations; located on the north-south line running from Aberdeen, South Dakota, to Sioux City and other Iowa points, it was the jumping-off point for the extension west to Chamberlain and the Black Hills terminal of Rapid City. Another branch extended east from Mitchell into northern Iowa to join the network of Milwaukee lines in that region.   (Collection of Dr. S. R. Wood)

THREE MILES WEST OF HARTLEY, these four Milwaukee Road engines were marooned in a deep drift amid the prairie cornfields. The two engines shown above on their way to rescue this stalled power were wrecked in the same snow-packed cut, making six engines all stuck in the same drift; the six locomotives were isolated there for three days before finally being dug out of their snowy prison.

A BRACE OF MILWAUKEE ROAD ENGINES dash through the yards in Hartley, Iowa, about the turn of the century, the wedge plow on the leading locomotive sending a cloud of powdery snow flying.

37

WINONA & ST. PETER RAILROAD was chartered on June 10, 1862, and constructed a standard gauge line that eventually reached from Winona, Minnesota, to Lake Kampeska (near Watertown) South Dakota. This system was 327 miles long, plus a branch line 3.75 miles in length from Mankato Junction to Mankato, Minnesota. The Mississippi River steamer KEOKUK delivered the first locomotive to the road at Winona on November 3, 1862; this engine was named the TIGER and was followed by others bearing such names as ROCHESTER, OWATONNA, MANKATO, UTICA, and KASSON. By 1866 the road had ten engines in service, running both freight and passenger equipment. The Winona & St. Peter was later acquired by the Chicago & North Western Railway, the latter concern having been organized in 1859 to operate the bankrupt Chicago, St. Paul & Fond du Lac Railroad. This photograph, dating back to 1881, shows a sextet of balloon-stacked wood-burners arrayed beyond the "strong-arm" turntable at the four-stall brick roundhouse located at Waseca, Minnesota. Waseca is located between Owatonna and St. Peter, not far east of the New Ulm region where the Sioux Indians massacred many inhabitants in the uprising of August, 1862. Construction on the old Winona & St. Peter was under way when 38 Sioux ringleaders, captured after the raids, were publicly hanged at Mankato, Minnesota, on December 26, 1862.

(Chicago & North Western Ry. photo, courtesy of Association of American Railroads)

TERRIFIC CORNFIELD MEET took place on the Peninsula Division of the Chicago & North Western a mile west of Hermansville, Michigan, in 1881. The operating rules in effect at the time gave westbound trains the right of track for 40 minutes beyond their schedule time, and on this day a schedule that operated only once a week was churning along behind C&NW Engine 278, a 4-4-0 built by Baldwin in 1872. Engineer Charles Seeney was at the throttle of the 278 and the weekly train was skippered by Conductor John J. Greene. The eastbound train, shown here at right, was headed by Engine No. 3 of the Winona & St. Peter Railroad, a C&NW subsidiary. This engine was known as the "Big Three," being the largest in service on the Division; she was a 4-4-0 built by Smith & Jackson in 1862. Engineer Joseph Frozier and Conductor Milton Pelton overlooked the weekly westbound and this spectacular pile-up was the result. Miraculously, no one was injured in the smash, probably because both crews joined the birds as the two balloon stackers bore down on each other. Note the little wooden ore cars scrambled amid the wreckage. In 1882 the C&NW 278 was renumbered Winona & St. Peter No. 44, later becoming C&NW 1044 in 1901. The 3-Spot was scrapped about 1888.   (Collection of Dr. S. R. Wood)

CHICAGO & NORTH WESTERN'S ENGINE 536 at Sleepy Eye, Minnesota, after a hard day of bucking snow during the harsh winter of 1887. This faded old photo was given to Dr. S. R. Wood by an uncle who served as a trainman on the Minnesota Division and was promoted to conductor in 1887. The uncle's vivid recollections of the hazardous operations of bucking snow are recounted in the text of this book and detail the methods used by this particular road to keep the line open during the blizzards. On one occasion the snowplow engine was running across the open prairie on her way to buck out some drifts when, without warning, she left the rails. Fortunately, the ground at the site of the derailment was fairly level and frozen so hard that the engine remained upright and continued to run along on the solid surface for a considerable distance before she could be halted, clipping off some 50 or 60 fence posts along the right-of-way as she rambled along without the benefit of rails under her wheels. Engine 536 was a 4-4-0 built by Schenectady, Shop No. 1798, in September, 1883, and was scrapped in 1913. Note the masses of snow packed on her boiler and against her cab, mute testimony of the deep drifts and frigid temperature. The hose connected to a valve on her steam dome provided live steam for thawing frozen ice and snow out of her valve gear and link blocks.   (Collection of Dr. S. R. Wood)

TERRIBLE WINTER OF 1887 wrought havoc with railroad operations throughout the West. This view shows a passenger train headed by Engine 5 of the Winona & St. Peter Railroad after the stalled train had been dug out of a deep snowdrift near Sleepy Eye, Minnesota. The Winona & St. Peter, a subsidiary of the Chicago & North Western, was especially hard hit by the fury of the blizzards that swept the northern plains. Some 15 locomotives of the road ended up in the ditch that winter, derailed by the heavy drifts. The line was so hampered by the snow and extreme cold that most of these locomotives were left lying where they had fallen, no attempt to rescue them being made until the spring thaw caused the weather to moderate. Engine 5 was a 4-4-0 built in the Chicago & North Western shops in 1880 and originally was the C&NW's No. 67. In August of 1887 she was assigned to the subsidiary Winona & St. Peter and given road number 5, which she bore until 1900 when she was changed back to the C&NW roster and became No. 893. The locomotive was sold in 1909.

(Collection of Dr. S. R. Wood)

CHICAGO & NORTH WESTERN'S ENGINE 388, new from the C&NW Shops in 1880, was involved in this minor mishap at Stanwood, Iowa, in the same year. Stanwood, located 51 miles west of Clinton, was the junction point of the original Chicago, Iowa & Nebraska Railroad with the Stanwood & Tipton Railroad. The Stanwood & Tipton, organized in 1872, built 8.5 miles of road from Stanwood south to Tipton, Iowa, in the same year it was organized and immediately began operations. The branch was leased to the Chicago & North Western, along with several other Iowa lines. The Stanwood & Tipton, a standard gauge pike laid with 56 pound rail, was a branch of the Chicago, Iowa & Nebraska, although organized and operated as a separate company. The Toledo & Northwestern Railroad, a branch of the Cedar Rapids & Missouri River Railroad opened in 1870, also came under the control of the Chicago & North Western. Later construction and acquisitions gave the C&NW connections to many Iowa towns, including What Cheer, Des Moines, Mason City, Alton, Sioux City, and Iowa Falls. Expansion west of the Missouri carried the road to Lander, Wyoming, via Casper and Fetterman, named in honor of early Army officers; from Dakota Junction, near Chadron, Nebraska, a line north to the Black Hills connected at Rapid City with the network of C&NW lines that cross-hatched South Dakota and the southern section of Minnesota.

(Collection of Dr. S. R. Wood)d

CHICAGO & NORTH WESTERN RAILWAY gained entry to the rich farmlands of Iowa through control of a series of early short line companies. Entering the state at Clinton, the first section of 82 miles carried the line to Cedar Rapids over the Chicago, Iowa & Nebraska Railroad. The line from Cedar Rapids west to a point on the east bank of the Missouri River, opposite Omaha, Nebraska, was built by the Cedar Rapids & Missouri River Railroad. Incorporated in the mid-1850's, the 271 miles of track between terminals was completed in 1866. This line was a vital supply link between the East and Omaha when the Union Pacific Railroad was constructing the transcontinental road west to a connection with the Central Pacific. The Chicago & North Western also operated the old Iowa Midland Railway, a road about 69 miles long that extended from Lyons to Anamosa, Iowa. This road, completed to Anamosa in October of 1871, was linked to the main line by a 2.6 mile branch from Clinton to Lyons. Pictured here at Clinton, Iowa, in the mid-1890's is Engine 220 of the Chicago & North Western. The big 4-4-0, a beautiful example of Schenectady's "Fast Mail," and her blower is urging the fire, raising a head of steam. The fireboy is looking back for the highball that will send the Mail on its way. Note the brakes applied to No. 220's spoked engine trucks.

(Courtesy of Fred Jukes)

MINNESOTA WESTERN RAILROAD was chartered in 1853 to construct a railway in Minnesota Territory, but the project never laid a foot of track. In 1870, sparked by "General" W. D. Washburn, the Minneapolis & St. Louis Railway Company was formed to take over the project of the defunct Minnesota Western. Construction started at Minneapolis on a route south via Sioux City Junction to Albert Lea, Minnesota. The connection was made with the St. Paul & Sioux City road at the Junction and a grand excursion opened the new route on November 25, 1871. The M&StL had, through it's subsidiary Minneapolis & Duluth Railroad, opened a short line from Minneapolis to White Bear Lake in July of 1871, providing a direct route north to Duluth via the connection with the Lake Superior & Mississippi Railroad at White Bear Lake. In a series of financial moves, the Minneapolis & St. Louis and the Minneapolis & Duluth were leased to the Lake Superior & Mississippi in 1871, and the first motive power used on both roads was furnished by the lessor. It was not until 1873 that the M&StL acquired two second-hand woodburners from the Northern Pacific; these engines were named W. D. WASHBURN and H. T. WELLES, in honor of the two guiding geniuses of the road. "Louie's" Engine 11 was a 4-4-0 built by Baldwin in 1879, Shop No. 4740. Shown here getting under way with a passenger train, she sports a straight stack which probably replaced an original diamond stack.

(Collection of Dr. S. R. Wood)

CYLINDER COCKS SPURTING STEAM, the Minneapolis & St. Louis switcher 53 poses in a snow-covered yard, aided by her crew in toggery designed to keep out winter's chill. The little diamond stacked 0-4-0 was built in November, 1881, by the Manchester Locomotive Works, Shop No. 942. Note the four-wheeled short tender in use with this yard engine. The lease of the M&StL to the Lake Superior & Mississippi had thrown the line under control of the Northern Pacific, but the panic of 1873 had caused the failure of Jay Cooke & Co., the N.P. backers, and in 1874 the "Louie" was returned to the original owners. These Minneapolis millers and business men soon pushed work on the extension of the south line and in November of 1877 the end of track reached Albert Lea. At this point a junction was made with the newly-completed Burlington, Cedar Rapids & Northern, an Iowa line backed by John I. Blair. Over this connection, freight from Minneapolis could now flow south over a series of connecting lines to St. Louis. Despite the great grasshopper plague of 1873 and the hardships imposed by the Granger laws, the grain and lumber trade boomed on the Minneapolis & St. Louis and goats such as No. 53 were kept busy marshalling the flow of traffic handled by American Standard road engines.

(Collection of Dr. S. R. Wood)

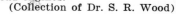

"MISERY & SHORT LIFE" was the nickname hung on the Minneapolis & St. Louis by the old-time boomer railroaders that roamed the West. The line acquired the Fort Dodge & Fort Ridgeley Railroad built in the late 1870's, and by means of an extension southwest from Albert Lea, Minnesota, and absorption of the subsidiary Minnesota & Iowa Southern, the M&StL was soon running trains to Fort Dodge, Iowa. By January of 1882, the line had built on south to Angus, heart of a rich coal producing area. The year 1882 also saw the road extended via Winthrop to Morton, Minnesota, on a new westward extension around the southern edge of Lake Minnetonka. Under a paper-work company called the Wisconsin, Minnesota & Pacific Railway, the network of rails was extended west from Morton to Watertown, South Dakota, a distance of 122 miles; this branch was completed in 1884. For a time the M&StL operated the Cannon Valley line, the old Minnesota Central road from Red Wing to Mankato, via Northfield and Waterville. The extension west past Lake Minnetonka brought a flood of passenger traffic to the resort area, and a regular shuttle train ran between Minneapolis and Excelsior; Engine 7, a small 4-4-0, handled this run and her engineer, Billy Watson, carried his pet Scotch terrier on the seatbox with him as they hustled pleasure-seekers, tourists, boating enthusiasts, fishermen, and vacationers to the lovely lake. Engine 61, built by Manchester in 1881, was typical of the main line locomotives in use on the M&StL at the time; she later was No. 123.
(Collection of Dr. S. R. Wood)

"THE HOOK AND EYE" was the appellation hung on the old Central Railroad of Iowa by the boomers of yesteryear, the cognomen having its origin in a company emblem in which the letter "C" ensnares the letter "I" near its top, buttonhook fashion. Parentage of the line dated back to 1868, when the Eldora Railroad & Coal Company completed a 16 mile road from Eldora to Ackley, Iowa. This road passed to the Iowa River Railway in September, 1868, and the new road began to build south. Late in 1869 the project was taken over by the Central Railroad of Iowa and on January 7, 1870, the pike was formally opened to Marshalltown. Construction was pushed from both ends and by 1872 the road was in operation to Northwood, near the Minnesota State Line, and south as far as Albia, Iowa, where it joined the St. Louis, Kansas City & Northern. The road was tossed into receivership in 1876 and controlled by Receiver Joseph B. Grinnel, emerging in May of 1879 as the Central Iowa Railway. Much of the road from Oskaloosa to Albia used the old grade thrown up by the Central Iowa Rail Road of 1865, a project of David Morgan and Peter Melendy that never got into operation. Engine 41 of the Central Iowa Railway is shown here at the Albia terminus in the 1880's. The 4-4-0 was built by Manchester, Shop No. 1070, in August of 1882. She later was Iowa Central's No. 115, then became Minneapolis & St. Louis No. 164. Note the arm on the bell bracket supporting the handrail, a Manchester characteristic.
(Collection of Dr. S. R. Wood)

MINNEAPOLIS & ST. LOUIS RAILROAD passed into receivership in 1888, being reorganized in 1894 as the Minneapolis & St. Louis Railway. Edwin Hawley became president of the new company in 1896 and expanded the line considerably. The "Louie" purchased the 20 miles of track belonging to the Minneapolis, New Ulm & Southern in 1899 and built an extension southwest to Storm Lake, Iowa, a distance of about 135 miles; this projection w a s headed for Omaha, but never got beyond Storm Lake, reaching there in 1900. Hawley gained control of the Iowa Central and it was operated in close connection with the M&StL, being formally purchased by the latter in 1912. In 1905 a subsidiary road, the Minnesota, Dakota & Pacific Railway was formed and a two-pronged western extension built from Watertown to Leola, South Dakota, and to LeBeau, a rip-snorting cattle town on the east bank of the muddy Missouri River; the Leola and LeBeau branches joined at Conde. Lack of business forced abandonment of the LeBeau line in 1940, and the projected westward lines from that ill-fated town and from Leola were destined to never materialize. On the main stem of the M&StL, the crack CANNON BALL EXPRESS of the '90's and the later NORTH STAR LIMITED fast passenger service from the Twin Cities to Chicago, via "Louie" connections which included the Rock Island and the Illinois Central. Power for the early varnish was furnished by trim 4-4-0's, such as the 67 shown here at Albert Lea in 1892, with Engr. E. Mead and his fireboy, Martin Engman. The 67 was a Manchester of 1881 vintage, later M&StL 129.   (Collection of Dr. S. R. Wood)

CENTRAL IOWA RAILWAY expanded its trackage by the acquisition of a number of short lines in the Buckeye State. The New Sharon, Coal Valley & Eastern Railway, incorporated in 1880, passed to the Chicago, Burlington & Pacific Railroad in January of 1882 and was purchased by the Central Iowa in April, 1882, giving the road a connection from Oskaloosa to a point on the Mississippi River opposite Keithsburg Illinois. Another short branch acquired from the Chicago, Burlington & Pacific extended from Newton to New Sharon, Iowa. The branch to Montzeuma, built by the Grinnel & Montezuma Railway, was gathered up by the Keithburg, Grinnell & Dakota Railway; this latter concern built a line from Newburg to State Center, Iowa, and both branches became Central Iowa properties in 1882. Added in the same year was the Iowa Central & Northwestern Railway's line from Minerva Junction to Story City. Sub-standard wages, coupled with poor track and rough operating conditions, made the Hook & Eye a boomer's pike, the proverbial "last chance" of those roaming railroaders who could not find employment on other roads. The labor turnover was fantastic, yet the boomers and a handful of homeguards maintained some tight schedules on the road in spite of hilly terrain light iron, dirt ballast and sharp curve. Typical motive power was represented by the Central's Engine 48, a Manchester 4-4-0 built in 1882 under Shop No. 1077. Renumbered Iowa Central 124, she later became the M&StL 154, Class D-8. The Central Iowa was favored by the Quakers for their annual Meeting treks to Oskaloosa.   (Collection of Dr. S. R. Wood)

IOWA CENTRAL RAILWAY emerged from the forclosed Central Iowa lines in 1888 and Cooke turned out Engine 60 for the new company in 1889. Bearing Shop No. 1975 the goat had a novel footboard arrangement, with double footboards being located fore and aft of her pilot beam. Eastbound traffic over the road from Oskaloosa crossed the bridge over the Mississippi at Keithsburg, completed in 1886, and ran to Peoria, Illinois, over a subsidiary line. From 1890 to 1897, the president of the Iowa Central was Russell Sage. The man was scorned by many for his miserly habits, but his name on the letter-boards of Engine 10 was a welcome sight to the employees since this engine usually hauled the pay car. Under the Sage regime, the Centreville, Moravia & Albia Railroad was purchased, extending the Iowa Central south to Centreville, (Centerville) Iowa. The old Hook & Eye road officially became a part of the Minneapolis & St. Louis in 1912. Time in its flight has eradicated the names of those who labored on the storied pike, but the name of an agent-operator on the absorbing M&StL is now a household word throughout the nation. Richard W. Sears, who once pounded the telegraph key at Lake Mills, Iowa, and later at North Redwood, Minnesota, peddled a shipment of watches refused by a local jeweler and started a mail order business after his first venture proved successful. In 1886 he quit the railroad, moved to Minneapolis, and in 1887 went to Chicago. Acquiring Alvah C. Roebuck as a partner, he built the famous firm of Sears, Roebuck & Company, probably the largest mail-order concern in the world.   (Collection of Dr. S. R. Wood)

TRAGEDY IN THE LAND OF 10,000 LAKES

Brainerd, Minnesota, was the site of this bad pile-up in 1882 when Northern Pacific's Engine 723 crashed into switch engine No. 76. The Mogul lies atop the debris, the tank of the goat can be noted at lower left. (Courtesy of Ronald V. Nixon)

Northern Pacific's Train No. 12, headed by Engine 716 (at left) collided head-on with N.P. Extra 424, westbound, near Baxter, Minnesota, on October 22, 1902. Force of the collision has torn the 716's boiler loose from the front end of the frame and saddle.
(Courtesy of Ronald V. Nixon)

Chicago & North Western's Engine 345, a Baldwin 4-6-0, plunged through this bridge east of Sanborn, Minnesota, on July 21, 1910. Relief engine 197, a Schenectady 4-6-0 built in 1899, at upper left. (Collection of Dr. S. R. Wood)

BUSY SANTA FE TERMINAL was located at Nickerson, Kansas, in the northern portion of Reno County. This historic photograph, taken in 1886, shows the 28-stall enginehouse and shops in the hey-day of their operation; note the locomotive standing near the cinder pits in the foreground, and the large supply of coal stacked in the open at the right of the cinder cars. Trees have been planted in the plot at the right of the office building to provide shade and a touch of color, while the level Kansas plain stretches away to the horizon in monotonous infinity. The Nickerson shops were removed to the old trail town of Newton, Kansas, around 1898. Nickerson was named in honor of Thomas Nickerson, the Bostonian who was president of the Santa Fe from 1874 until 1880.

(Courtesy of Santa Fe Railway)

The Central Plains.

The first engines to chuff along the eastern reaches of the old Mississippi were puny by modern standards, and quaint to look upon. Huge stacks topped their dinky boilers, and their tenders were piled high with fuel wood, while the mechanical refinements they lacked were made up for by gaudy trim, tasteful paintings, and a lavish use of shining brass ornamentation. Their flanges screeched over light-weight iron rail and in their wake rolled the trains of flimsy wooden cars and coaches, trussed with rods and coupled with the man-killing old link and pin. Brave were the men who manned these primitive trains and equally brave were the passengers who fared forth aboard them. Wrecks were commonplace, boiler explosions not infrequent, and accidents of a wide variety beset the early trains and travelers.

HISTORY MAKER, this woodburning 4-4-0 named the MISSOURI was one of the two original locomotives operated on the Hannibal & St. Joseph Railroad, the first line to reach the Missouri River. The company was organized in 1852 and completed from Hannibal to St. Joseph, Missouri, in 1859. In 1860 the road put in a bid for the U.S. Mail service formerly carried by river steamboats and staged a record speed run that won the Government mail contract; the special train that ran the speed trials was drawn by the old MISSOURI. In July, 1862, this same engine hauled the first railway post office cars on their east bound maiden voyage between St. Joseph and West Quincy. The Hannibal & St. Joseph line later became a part of the Chicago, Burlington & Quincy.   (C.B.&Q. photo, courtesy of Association of American Railroads)

West of the great river, the troubles of railroaders were destined to be multiplied. The threat of Indian attacks was very real, and the forces of Nature conspired to assault the Iron Horse with blizzards, sand storms, and floods in magnitudes such as Easterners had never dreamed of.

Yet in spite of such opposition, the brawny track gangs kept spiking rails into the sunset and the bewhiskered crews rolled their trains along these iron highways, undaunted by Hell or high water. Companies rose and fell, the pay cars might be months over-due, trains ditched with monotonous regularity, yet the operating crews kept plugging away and their smoke plumes stained the far horizons.

It has been but little over a century ago that the railroads of the United States stretched west to the waters of the Mississippi River and commenced their invasion of the American West.

The first rails to arrive on the eastern shores of that great artery of river-borne commerce were those of the old Chicago & Rock Island Railroad, the road being opened for service between Chicago and Rock Island, Illinois, on July 10, 1854. In the following year, the Illinois Central, in connection with the Galena & Chicago, reached the great river, as did the lines of the Chicago & Alton Railroad, organized as the Chicago & Mississippi Railroad and chartered in 1847.

In 1856 the Chicago, Burlington & Quincy brought their rails to the Father of Waters, followed in 1858 by the old La Crosse & Milwaukee. The Mobile & Ohio, a broad gauge line, reached the river in 1859 and a direct and continuous north-south line from Chicago to New Orleans was opened in 1874. Memphis, Tennessee, was reached in 1857 by the Memphis & Charleston Railroad. The advent of these various lines and the network that sprang up in their wake soon began to make serious inroads on the steamboat traffic that churned the Missisippi, and the battle between railroaders and rivermen was not long in coming to a head.

The Rock Island completed the first railroad bridge across the Mississippi between Davenport, Iowa, and Rock Island, Illinois, on April 21, 1856, and on the following day the first engine, named the FORT DES MOINES, crossed the Howe truss structure. This bridge, 1,582 feet long, had a 285 foot draw span over the main channel to permit river steamers to pass through, the bridge itself being only about 35 feet above the mean water mark.

Steamboatmen, anxious to block the competing rail lines, had tried to halt construction of this bridge with court injunctions, but these had been over-ruled by the Supreme Court. On the night of May 6, 1856, the sidewheel packet EFFIE ALTON passed upstream through the open draw, then suddenly appeared to go out of control and swept back downstream, striking the span next to the open draw. Fire immediately broke out and destroyed the boat, along with one span of the bridge. The draw section was jammed and a heavy wind a few days after the fire sent it to the bottom of the river. Although the incident smacked of premeditated sabotage, the boatmen sued the railroad and won their damage suits in local courts, the Iowa judge declaring the bridge a menace to navigation and ordering the section on the Iowa side removed. The Rock Island engaged a young lawyer named Abraham Lincoln to defend the road, and although he lost the local trials, Lincoln won a reversal from the Supreme Court and the railroad was granted the right to bridge the river. The big bridge was restored to service in the following year and the river interests drew off to lick their wounds and watch the steam locomotives drive the floating river palaces and freight boats to the boneyards.

Railroad fever promptly gripped the Mississippi Valley and a multitude of projects were launched. Every major town and most of the jerkwater villages throughout the Mississippi drainage struggled for rail connections and some fantastic schemes were developed. Many of these projects never got beyond the paper stage, and some of the lines that were built were the result of the untiring perseverance of a few farsighted individuals who realized that the railways were destined to change the American way of life.

The change of transportation methods was not accomplished overnight, nor without opposition. Stage and freight line outfits joined with the steamboat faction in combatting the railways, for in the swift passage of the locomotive they saw the doom of their slow and often unreliable vehicles. The transition from horsepower to steam called for many adjustments, but in the end the railroads triumphed and brought about a system of standardization previously undreamed of. One of the greatest changes, insofar as effect upon the general public was concerned, was the development of a system of standard time. Railway clocks and train schedules began to have a telling impact on American life, and the bonds of regimenta-

HANNIBAL & ST. JOSEPH RAILROAD was organized in 1852 and the road was completed on February 13, 1859. The main line, 206 miles in length, extended from the historic old Mississippi River town of Hannibal westwardly across the State of Missouri to St. Joseph, with branches extending from Palmyra, Missouri, to Quincy, Illinois, from Cameron, Missouri, south to Kansas City, and a 22 mile extension running southwesterly from St. Joseph to Atchison, Kansas. By 1878, the Hannibal & St. Jo had a roster of 79 locomotives operating under the supervision of Master Mechanic G. B. Simonds. Engine No. 56, shown here at St. Charles, Missouri, in 1889, was a 4-4-0 built for the road by the Grant Locomotive Works in 1872. Note the heavy car chain on the rear of her tank, suspended on hooks above the tool box; the frequent break-in-twos made this chain a necessity, and the sight of brakemen struggling along beneath its weight to chain a broken train together was a common one in earlier days of railroading. (Courtesy of Dr. S. R. Wood)

tion drew a notch closer.

The demand for more speed forced the railroads to improve their service and equipment, for the cream of the business went to the competing line that offered the speediest trains. The United States Government fostered this by awarding mail contracts to the winners of railroad speed trials. Oddly enough, safety on the rails lagged far behind, and it frequently developed that safety devices and practices were brought into being under the pressure of law, forced upon the railroads by the demands of an outraged public and by the united actions of the brotherhoods representing the employees.

Locomotive boiler inspections, improved brakes and couplers, railroad signals, and Government supervision of the conditions of track, structures, and equipment eventually put an end to the frightful sacrifice of human life and limb that had been accepted as commonplace in the struggling infancy of rail operations.

The Civil War wrecked some Western lines and boomed others, but the great era of expansion set in following the end of that senseless, bloody conflict. The boom period of the railroads' growth was the age of the robber barons and some of the great scandals centering around railroad manipulations rocked the nation.

Politics and chicanery often decided the courses of various roads, frequently to the detriment of the region served, and many lines became the pawns of the financial giants who looted and plundered on vast scales.

The photos and accompanying captions in this book may help to capture some of the spirit of high adventure that permeated the West in the wake of the steam locomotive. In such a limited space it has been possible to hit only the highlights of a few of the myriad operating companies, but the photographs tell a story of a fascinating way of life now vanished, one that in all probability will never return to the American scene.

Following the close of the Civil War, many communities in the Western border states began clamoring for rail transportation. Promoters had a field day and townsites boomed and busted as the fortunes of the numerous infant railways rose and fell. In many instances the cost of railroad construction was prohibitive and various cost-cutting methods were employed. In 1875 the Farmers' Union Railroad was incorporated to construct a 300 mile narrow gauge line across Iowa, from the Mississippi to the Missouri. In the first year of its existence, the road constructed about 12 miles of track from Liscomb to Beaman and put 1 locomotive and 10 freight cars in service. To keep construction costs within reach of their limited finances, the Farmers' Union Railroad laid this trackage with wooden rails; hard maple stringers $3\frac{1}{2}$ by 6 inches were used for this purpose, notched into the ties and keyed in place. This wooden rail was expected to last for about 4 years, by which time the road's officials hoped to be able to replace the wooden rail with the conventional iron or steel.

The Iowa Eastern Railroad was another corn belt pike that got under way with difficulty. It was incorporated in 1871 with the intent of

A DAINTY DIAMOND STACK, set high atop a short smokebox, graced Engine 33 of the Kansas City, St. Joseph & Council Bluffs Railroad. The Manchester 4-4-0 was built in October, 1879, and bore Shop No. 775; she is shown here at St. Joseph, Missouri, on November 6, 1888. This engine was acquired by the Chicago, Burlington & Quincy in 1898 and given CB&Q No. 533. Note the arrow shaped target on the stub switch stand in the right foreground. (Courtesy of Dr. S R. Wood)

KANSAS CITY, ST. JOSEPH & COUNCIL BLUFFS RAILROAD was formed in April. 1870, by a series of consolidations of smaller lines. The Council Bluffs & St. Joseph R.R. and the St Joseph & Council Bluffs R.R. consolidated under the latter name in 1868 and their joint line opened for traffic early in 1869. In April, 1870, the Missouri Valley Railroad joined the fold, and the road was then reorganized as the Kansas City, St. Joseph & Council Bluffs, linking Kansas City, Missouri, with Council Bluffs, Iowa, with 199 miles of standard gauge track. In addition to the main stem, the road had a 50 mile branch from Amazonia, Missouri, to a connection with the CB&Q at Hopkins, on the Iowa State Line; the company also operated the St. Joseph & Topeko Railroad, a 25 mile line from St. Joseph to Atchison, Kansas, under a lease. Engine 7 of the KCStJ&CB, a pretty 4-4-0 Manchester of 1869 bearing Shop No. 154, is shown here at St. Joseph, Missouri, on March 14, 1886.
(Courtesy of Dr. S. R. Wood)

building 200 miles of narrow gauge track from Beulah to Des Moines, Iowa, via Elkader. Some 15 miles of track was put down in the summer of 1872 and the road was placed in operation in October. A baggage car served as the depot at Beulah and the business at the south end of the line was carried on in a tent. The road had no turntable, no engine house, no water tank, and box cars. When the harvest season approached, the railroaders solved the box car problem by building sides and tops on 16 flat cars, but all the grain was handled in sacks, as it had to be transhipped by hand to the standard gauge cars of the Chicago, Milwaukee & St. Paul road at the Beulah interchange. In spite of all the hardships and lack of equipment, the little pike delivered 100 cars of freight to the Milwaukee during December, 1872, and as soon as the weather permitted, the road was extended. Wooden rails were used on the Iowa Eastern, 1½ miles being laid in 1874 and in 1875 the line laid 3½ miles of wooden rail and 1 mile of light iron rail. Two locomotives chuffed over the fertile route, and by 1875 the road boasted

2 passenger and 31 freight cars; by the close of 1876 the line covered 19½ miles and grossed a tidy $26,129.61. From such humble beginnings grew the present great rail network that serves the Mid-west. The Iowa Eastern was taken over by the Chicago, Milwaukee & St. Paul in 1882 and converted from 3 feet to the standard 4′8½″ of that line.

Other early narrow gauge lines in the region included the Kansas Central Railroad, the St. Louis, Keosauqua & St. Paul, the Des Moines & Minnesota, the Covington, Columbus & Black Hills, and the Wyandotte, Kansas City & North Western, to name but a few.

Railroaders in the region encountered many of the hardships found on the nation's railroads in the great era of expansion. Poor track, flimsy equipment, and lack of pay were all things to be taken in stride. The manual couplings crippled and maimed the employees in train and yard service, while boiler explosions, wrecks, and derailments were commonplace. Enginemen were subjected to many minor irritations; the wooden lagging applied to the boilers, beneath

STEAMBOAT LANDING AT OMAHA is depicted in this photograph taken about 1865. Freight cars of the infant Union Pacific stand on the levee at the left, awaiting the cargo delivered by the steamers operating on the Missouri River. At right is the big sidewheeler, COLORADO, a Hannibal & St. Joe Railroad packet; further upstream a twin-stacked stern-wheeler discharges cargo. Nearly all of the material used in construction of the early portions of the Union Pacific, including the locomotives, arrived here by river boat.   (Courtesy of Union Pacific Railroad)

the Russia iron jackets, frequently caught fire and sent eye-smarting smoke into the cab until the smouldering lagging could be doused with a bucket of water. The old style of tubular water glass frequently burst, filling the cab with steam and hot water and the flying fragments of glass that sometimes caused serious injuries.

An element of uncertainty existed regarding employment before the railroad brotherhoods remedied conditions. An employee might be discharged without any just cause, simply because some brass hat took a dislike to him or was offended by some minor action. When a new Master Mechanic was assigned to a division, he often brought along a number of his pet engine crews from his former location, and the older employees of the district would be fired for some imagined or trumped-up offenses, in order to create jobs for these transplanted favorites.

In spite of these drawbacks, the railroader carried on, displaying a pride in his calling that few other occupations could instill. Crews did their valiant best to get over the road, exerting their efforts when the nearest supervisory personnel might be miles away. This spirit of united effort is still a major factor in the operation of our nation's railroads, as strong today as it was in the era of balloon stacks and wood-burners.

Railroad men were no angels; they drank whiskey, gambled, swore fluently, and sinned luridly in the lusty days when the web of steel was spanning the frontier. The very nature of their environment created a rough and ready class of men, the weaklings rapidly falling by the wayside. Yet the calling became a respected one as civilization moved in the wake of their rowdy pioneering, and the majority of them became good citizens, building homes and rearing families. As rail operation became more settled, a caste system developed within the fraternity, with the gray-bearded passenger engineers and conductors as the upper strata. These individuals were the deans of the road, followed by the freight runners and skippers. They held a social distinction in their communities and were considered on a par with the local banker, doctor, and leading merchant.

The boomers who followed the various spurts of business also played an important role in the railroad game. Some of them were outlaws, black-listed from steady employment and hired only when no other help was obtainable. The majority of the boomers were of a better class, good railroad men with itchy feet who yearned to see what lay beyond the next mountain range. They followed the grain rushes in the prairie states, and the cattle rushes that created a heavy seasonal demand for extra trains. Migrating with the birds, they roamed the lines of the West, acquiring a high degree of ability in their various skills. The homeguard might secretly envy their freedom but stuck to his job, keeping the trains rolling when the boomer departed for milder climes.

Railroading was a tough school where an apt pupil might learn something every day yet never graduate.

Many officials rose from the ranks to guide the destinies of lines great and small, their places filled by others drawn to the adventurous life on the iron highroad. The prestige of running a locomotive was gained after years of toil, shovelling mountains of coal into roaring fireboxes. The dapper passenger conductor strolled the aisles of the coaches in comparative comfort, but the chances are that he had braved the elements on the slippery deck of the boxcars for many years before donning the blue serge and polished buttons.

Railroading was hard work, no job for weaklings or laggards. Brakemen muscled tons of freight at way stations, lugged car chains, draw bars, jacks, and journal brasses; they chilled at the lonely flagman's post behind their trains, in sight of the warm and cheery caboose but bound by the call of duty to keep their vigil until recalled by the whistle of the engine.

Living conditions at terminals away from home were often deplorable. The beds in dingy rooming houses frequently never grew cold, and the greasy food served in fly-infested beaneries would have taxed the digestive abilities of a goat. The knock of the call boy routed out crews in all the dark hours of the night, fair weather or foul, but the men responded and the trains moved.

Nurtured on hardships and consorting with danger, the railroad man created his own traditions and was justly proud of his craft. To these veterans of the rail our nation owes a lasting debt of gratitude.

TRUE WESTERN PIONEER was this funnel stacker of early design. The 4-4-0 shown here was built in October, 1853, as the ANTELOPE of the old Central Military Tract by the Amoskeag Manufacturing Company of Manchester, New Hampshire, a firm that built locomotives from 1849 to 1856. Bearing Amoskeag's Shop No. 83, she was an inside-connected woodburner, her cylinders and main rods being located inside her frames. The Central Military Tract Railroad became a part of the Chicago, Burlington & Quincy, and the ANTELOPE became No. 34 of the CB&Q; this view shows her posed on the bank of the Missouri River at White Cloud, Kansas, in August of 1872, headed south. Engineer David M. Beauchamp is seated at her throttle and Fireman John T. Weld stands in her gangway. At the time this photograph was taken, the ANTELOPE was running on the Atchison & Nebraska Railroad, a standard gauge line extending from Atchison, Kansas, to Lincoln, Nebraska, a distance of 148.89 miles. The Atchison & Nebraska was organized in 1870 and opened for service in 1872, later becoming the property of the Chicago, Burlington & Quincy. The Atchison & Nebraska Railroad was a close relative of the St. Joseph & Topeka Railroad, which extended from Atchison, Kansas, to St. Joseph, Missouri, serving as link with the Kansas City, St. Joseph & Council Bluffs Railroad. (Courtesy of Dr. S. R. Wood)

KANSAS CITY PASSENGER, this photograph taken in July of 1878 shows Train No. 1 of the Burlington & Missouri River at the ornate passenger station at Kansas City, Missouri. The varnished cars are headed by B&MR Engine 6, a graceful 4-4-0 named the NEBRASKA. The locomotive was built by Manchester in May, 1870, and carried Shop No. 257. Engineer Fred Thompson is shown here at the throttle, with Fireman W. E. Sullivan standing in the gangway; at left above the fireman's head can be seen the bell cord, connecting the coaches with a gong in the engine cab to enable the train crew to signal the enginemen. (Courtesy of Dr. S. R. Wood)

FIRST TRAIN INTO BROKEN BOW was hauled by Engine 120 of the Burlington & Missouri River Railroad. The 4-4-0 with the diamond stack is shown here about 1886 near the Nebraska city with the colorful name, standing on the approach to a short timber trestle, the raw earth of recent construction evident in the fill in the foreground. Note the man at far left, holding up the long length of Engine 120's pilot bar coupler; the feat of maintaining a safe balance on the scanty footing of the stave pilot and guiding the heavy metal rod into the socket of a link and pin draw-head while in motion was one that called for both strength and skill on the part of the old-time trainmen. (Courtesy of Denver Public Library's Western Collection)

BURLINGTON & MISSOURI RIVER RAILROAD was organized to carry the rails of the Chicago, Burlington & Quincy across the broad reaches of Nebraska. Manchester Locomotive Works built Engine No. 7 for the B & M R in 1870 at a cost of $11,500. The trim American Standard was named the WAUHOO and was rebuilt in the Burlington's Havelock shops in 1897. She was renumbered CB&Q 371 in 1904 and was retired from service in April, 1927.

(Courtesy of Chicago, Burlington & Quincy R.R.)

PLATTSMOUTH, NEBRASKA, located in Cass County, was the site of the shops of the old Burlington & Missouri River Railroad. The town was laid out on the south bank of the Platte River, where that stream flowed into the muddy waters of the Missouri. Across the Missouri River was the C. B. & Q.'s Iowa terminal, Pacific Junction, located in Mills County. Burlington & Missouri River Engine 35, a lovely 4-4-0 of graceful design and clean appearance, was built in the B.&M.R. Shops at Plattsmouth in 1881 and served the road well until she was scrapped on June 30, 1903. This rare old photo shows her posed on the shore of the great river that had provided the early trappers, explorers, and mountain men with their first highway into the vast regions of the American West. (Courtesy of Association of American Railroads)

MANCHESTER LOCOMOTIVE WORKS turned out this 4-4-0 for the Burlington & Missouri River Railroad in March, 1871. Bearing Shop No. 324, she was assigned B&MR No. 60 and was named the ARAPAHOE. This photo shows her in service on the road at Creston, Iowa, in 1873. The builders of this engine maintained a locomotive works in Manchester, New Hampshire, from around 1856 until 1901, when they joined with other builders to form the American Locomotive Company, with a main plant at Schenectady, New York. Included in the combine were Brooks Locomotive Works, Dickson Manufacturing Co., Cooke Locomotive & Machine Works, Schenectady Locomotive Works, Pittsburgh Locomotive & Car Works, Rhode Island Locomotive Works, Richmond Locomotive Works, and the Manchester firm; in 1905 the Rogers Locomotive Works was acquired by Alco, completing the formation of the powerful combine that absorbed the historic old group of engine builders.
(Courtesy of Dr. S. R. Wood)

THE FAST MAIL grew into an American legend and the flight of the speeding train captured the fancy of young and old alike. Graybeards gathered at wayside stations to marvel at the swift passage of the fabled train, and lads grew to manhood dreaming of the day that they might sit on that loftiest of thrones, the seatbox in the cab of the roaring engine that hurtled across the American West. The Burlington won the contract for carrying the transcontinental mails between Chicago and Council Bluffs in the glory years of steam railroading, inaugurating their "Fast Mail" in May, 1884. The mail contract was a thing to be jealously guarded, and nervy runners were chosen to make and hold the time with engines tuned to perfection. This 1897 photograph shows No. 550 of the Chicago, Burlington & Quincy tied onto four postal cars, streaking across the level prairies. Smoke streams back from the shotgun stack of the Belpaire-boilered 4-4-0 as she digests her coal and clips off the miles with her precious cargo, racing the sunset and heading toward immortality. The impersonal drone of the mail plane lost in the clouds can never rival the roar of the stack, the drumming drivers, and the lingering tang of coal smoke that marked the passing of the Fast Mail in her finest hour.
(Chicago, Burlington & Quincy Railroad photo, courtesy of the Association of American Railroads)

THE "Q" IN BURLINGTON is represented in this photograph taken at the Burlington, Iowa, passenger station in 1885. American Standard No. 134 of the Chicago, Burlington & Quincy heads a 3-car passenger consist while the bearded skipper and runner compare watches prior to departure. Lettering on the forward end of the baggage and express car informs all who care to read that this is also a "United States Railway Post Office." The Burlington was justly proud of their Government mail contracts and the "Fast Mail" has become a Burlington legend.
(Courtesy of Chicago, Burlington & Quincy Railroad)

KILPATRICK'S GRADING OUTFIT was busily engaged in hacking out the roadbed for the Burlington & Missouri River Railroad when the teamsters and their families posed for this picture. The location is in Custer County, Nebraska, on the line that presently will connect Lincoln with Billings, Montana; the Burlington steel crossed the northwestern section of Nebraska, cut through the southwestern tip of South Dakota's Black Hills, and led through the Wyoming badlands within sight of the famed Devil's Tower on the way west to Billings. Near the Crow Agency station, between Lodge Grass and Hardin, Montana, the Burlington trains pass near the battlefield where Custer's brave troopers traded their lives for immortality.
(Courtesy of the Chicago, Burlington & Quincy Railroad)

HEADED WEST, a high-stepping Atlantic thunders along under a plume of coal smoke with the "Denver Flyer" of the Chicago, Burlington & Quincy, cheered on her flight by the barefoot boy at the left. This grand action shot of the Burlington's Engine 1592 at speed was taken near Downer's Grove, Illinois, in 1899. The rangy 4-4-2 was capable of hustling the varnished cars through the lush flatlands at high speeds, hurrying passengers and mail toward their destinations in Denver, the former Cherry Creek diggings named in honor of General James W. Denver, the first Governor of Kanasas Territory. (Courtesy of the Chicago, Burlington & Quincy Railroad)

WRECKING CRANE No. 3 of the Burlington & Missouri River Railroad picks up the remains of a box car smashed in a wreck three miles west of Ord, Nebraska, on August 10, 1899. The wrecker, assigned to the Nebraska division, was typical of the big hooks of the day. It consisted of a platform car with a house at one end to enclose the vertical steam boiler and the engines and hoisting machinery; the long wooden spar pole and boom could be raised and lowered to facilitate moving the equipment. By means of purchase blocks, considerable weights could be lifted; the box car shown here is suspended clear of the ground, even though manila lines are being used instead of the steel wire cables of later days. Guy lines steadied the crane as it ponderously cleared away the debris from the all-too-frequent accidents that marred early Western rail operations.

THE UGLY DUCKLINGS pictured here show the incongruous results of an attempt to combine the diamond stacks of earlier days with the bulky motive power outshopped after the turn of the century. The two Consolidation types belonged to the Burlington & Missouri River Railroad, bore road numbers 3318 and 3319, and were built by Alco in 1903. This photograph was probably taken at Broken Bow, Nebraska. The tales spun by Burlington crews were recorded by Frank H. Spearman, a banker in the division point of McCook, Nebraska, and his railroad writing won him considerable fame; the authentic color captured by Spearman's pen from the working railroaders lives forever in his books, THE NERVE OF FOLEY, HELD FOR ORDERS, and WHISPERING SMITH, the latter story based on the war between the Union Pacific and the Hole-in-the-Wall gang of train robbers.

BURLINGTON ROUNDHOUSE FORCE posed for this photo at Alliance, Nebraska, around 1900. The crew and their canine mascot are shown with Engine 312 of the Burlington & Missouri River Railroad. The 4-6-0 coal burner with the shotgun stack was built by Rogers in 1892, had 64 inch drivers, and tipped the scales at about 110 tons when loaded with coal and water. Note the boiler extending back through the wooden cab on this Class K-2 tenwheeler.

(Courtesy of the Chicago, Burlington & Quincy Railroad)

PIONEER CAR FERRY, this 1871 photograph depicts the Missouri River Transfer boat, H. C. NUTT, a big Mississippi-style sidewheeler, at the Union Pacific landing at Omaha, Nebraska. A diamond stacked locomotive is pulling a string of freight cars up the apron at the landing after they have been ferried across the river from Council Bluffs, Iowa. This ferry service was used until the big railroad bridge over the Missouri was placed in service in 1872. Figures and arrows indicate: 1, St. Philomena's Cathedral; 2, Cozzen's House, built by the noted George Francis Train; 3, Canfield House; 4, Union Pacific Headquarters, formerly Herndon House; 5, Omaha's first High School.   (Courtesy of Union Pacific Railroad)

SPANNING THE BIG MUDDY, this is the first Union Pacific Railroad permanent bridge built across the Missouri River at Omaha. The structure, linking the Nebraska terminus with Council Bluffs, Iowa, was first opened for traffic in 1872 Prior to that time, all rail traffic was ferried across the river, or moved over on the temporary timber trestling erected whenever the stream froze solidly in winter. The large white building, visible under the third span from the right, housed a saloon, conveniently located near the railroad tracks running under the bridge in the foreground.

(Courtesy of Union Pacific Railroad)

TRANSCONTINENTAL TERMINUS, this view taken around 1870 shows the roundhouse and shops of the Union Pacific located at Omaha, Nebraska. All supplies and equipment were brought to Omaha by boat, or ferried across the Missouri River from Council Bluffs, Iowa, until the big bridge was built in 1872. The exception to this was the occasion when the river froze over and temporary piling, driven through holes cut in the ice, carried the trains across on a wooden trestle that was removed before the spring thaws set in.   (Courtesy of Union Pacific Railroad)

WINNING THE WEST, the locomotives of the Union Pacific paved the way for settlers and civilization between the Missouri and the Great Salt Lake. No creation of man has so captured the fancy as the steam locomotive and the graceful lines of the engines constructed between 1860 and the end of the century are thought by many to be the most pleasing ever to emerge from the drawing boards. A prime example of this captivating style was Union Pacific's Engine, 82, a 4-4-0 built by Hinkley & Williams in 1868. This American Standard had 17 x 24 inch cylinders and 54 inch drivers, the engine alone weighing 54,000 pounds. This photograph was taken when the 82 was in helper service between Echo, Utah, and Evanston, Wyoming; note the hewn ties and poorly-ballasted track, and the crooked, splintered sticks of cottonwood fuel piled on her decorated tank. Railroading in the era was a young man's game, as indicated by the youthful appearance of the runner with his arm draped nonchalantly over the 82's valve stem. The hazards of operation cut down many railroaders in their prime and of the many boys who climbed aboard the iron horse only a few survived the dangerous conditions to become greybeards. Wrecks, explosions, accidents, and exposure took a high toll and the graveyards of the West are heavily populated with those brave men who cashed in while keeping the wheels rolling.

(Courtesy of Union Pacific Railroad)

HELL ON WHEELS. As the construction gangs of the Union Pacific thrust the rails west, stringing steel toward the setting sun, a motley and turbulent crowd of camp followers traveled in their wake. Portable saloons, bagnios, dining halls, and other businesses were moved from one railhead to the next in order to cater to the swarms of workmen. This view shows a semi-permanent camp at Bear River City, Wyoming Territory, located on White Sulphur Creek some 965 miles west of Omaha. Signs identify such establishments as the "R.R. Restaurant," New England Restaurant," "Club Room," "J. E. Mahan, Liquors," "Union Bakery," "Washing & Ironing," and the "Rail Road Saloon." The portable darkroom of the photographer can be seen in the rear of the wagon at the left.

(Courtesy of Union Pacific Railroad)

WATER SUPPLY for Union Pacific locomotives and terminals was one of the many problems encountered as the road built west. This huge windmill pumped water for the railroad at Laramie, Wyoming Territory, and cost a reported $10,000. A 4-4-0 with diamond stack is shown at the tank, with the roundhouse and shops visible in the right background.
(Courtesy of Union Pacific Railroad)

UNION PACIFIC YARD CREWS lined up with their switch engines at Rock Springs, Wyoming, for this photo taken on October 2, 1895. Engines 1111, at left, and 1106, at right, are both 0-6-0 goats built by Baldwin in 1890; they had 71 x 24 inch cylinders and 51 inch driving wheels. Engine 1289, center, is an old deckless hog built by Taunton in 1883 as the Union Pacific's No. 273. She had 20 x 24 inch cylinders and 50 inch drivers; these early Consolidation types were used in road service between Ogden and Evanston and between Cheyenne and Laramie, on the hill districts of the Union Pacific. The crews shown here switched under the supervision of Yardmaster P. Tobin, standing at right in white shirt and vest. Engineer E. Smythes and Fireman J. Murphy manned the "four aces," Eng. 1111, with Foreman J. Hansen and Switchmen R. Seaton and J. B. Sears; J. Murphy and F. Palmer were the engine crew on the 1289, with Foreman M. Nicholson and Switchmen G. Demerest and C. Cousins; the 1106 was in charge of Engr. D. P. Murphy and Fireman J. Gillespie, with Foreman H. H. Still and his switchmen, Chas. Ontsen and T. Brannigan. It is interesting to note the predominance of Irish names in the roster of these crews.
(Courtesy of Union Pacific Railroad)

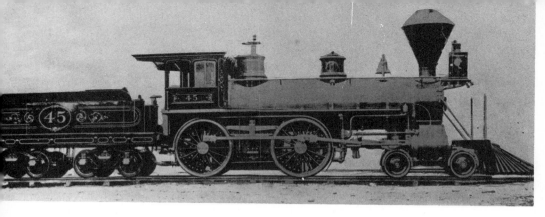

Engine 45 was built by the Grant Locomotive Works in 1867, had 16 x 24 inch cylinders and 61 inch drivers. She was sold to the Oregon Short Line in 1882.

A Gallery Of Union Pacific Locomotives

Engine 90 was a Baldwin 4-6-0 built in 1868 and is shown here in front of the Philadelphia works. She had 16 x 24 inch cylinders, 54 inch drivers, and was scrapped in 1899.

Engine 235 was a 4-6-0 built by Taunton in 1881 with 18 x 24 inch cylinders and 56 inch drivers. She went to the Oregon Short Line around 1883.
(All photos courtesy of Union Pacific Railroad)

Engine 815 was originally No. 166, a Taunton 4-4-0 built in 1875. Rebuilt in 1886, she is shown here near the Council Bluffs, Iowa, roundhouse around 1900, while in service on Trains 42 and 43, Council Bluffs to Beatrice.

Engine 268 was a Taunton 2-8-0 built in 1883 with 20 x 24 inch cylinders and 50 inch drivers. She is shown here minus her headlight at the Taunton factory prior to delivery.

Engine 1807 was built by New York Loco. Works, Rome, N.Y., in 1890. Her 69 inch drivers and 20 x 24 inch cylinders gave her plenty of speed. She is pictured here at Rock Springs, Wyoming; note the jacket covering her smokebox.

(All photos courtesy Union Pacific Railroad)

Union Pacific 202 was built by Danforth & Cooke in 1880. She had no engine brakes, but tank brake wheel and rigging are visible here.

Union Pacific 177 was built by Taunton in 1878, had 18 x 24 inch cylinders and 57 inch drivers. She was later renumbered 936.

Union Pacific 768 was designed by Clement Hackney, Supt. of Motive Power, and built by Rogers in 1887-88. She was a camelback with a Wooten firebox, rebuilt to a conventional engine in the Omaha Shops after failing to burn slack coal efficiently, and was one of a group of 10 engines of this type.   (All photos, courtesy of Union Pacific Railroad)

EXCELLENT SPECIMEN OF PHOTOGRAPHER'S ART is this view of Union Pacific's Engine 553, taken at Columbus, Nebraska, about 1882, with Engineers James D. Taylor standing by the wooden stave pilot. Built by Danforth, Cooke & Company in 1866, the 4-4-0 was originally Union Pacific No. 10 and bore the name DENVER; her sister engine, No. 11, was named the COLORADO. The Union Pacific paid $15,450 for the engine when she was built, and she had been worked over in the Union Pacific Shops when this detailed photograph was taken. Note the ornate bell stand and the cages on the front of her smokebox, applied to hold the signal lamps. This engine was built with 16 x 24 inch cylinders and weighed 75,300 pounds She was vacated from the U.P. roster in January, 1902.   (Courtesy of Union Pacific Railroad)

COLUMBUS, NEBRASKA, ROUNDHOUSE forms the backdrop for this view of Union Pacific's No. 567 and crew. The 4-4-0 was originally Union Pacific No. 41, built in 1867 by Taunton, but had been rebuilt when this photo was taken, prior to her scrapping in 1899. Her specifications included 17 x 24 inch cylinders, 63 inch drivers, and a total weight of 76,500 pounds; her tender held 6 tons of coal and 1,780 gallons of water. The fireman, standing by the gangway, holds the traditional old tallow pot that gave that nickname to members of his craft.   (Courtesy of Union Pacific Railroad)

THREE AMERICAN STANDARDS lined up for this view at the Union Pacific roundhouse at Columbus, Nebraska, in 1888. At left is No. 719, a Brooks engine built in 1886; next is No. 78, a diamond stacker built by Schenectady in 1867-68 and originally Union Pacific's No. 23; at right is No. 505, a Danforth & Cooke 4-4-0 built in 1868 as Union Pacific's No. 86 and scrapped in 1899. This picture was presented to the Union Pacific Historical Museum by Mr. I. N. "Dick" Wright, who retired as a locomotive engineer after 45 years of service; some of the men identified are, left to right: 7th, Tom Wilson, hostler; 11th, Engr. John Shehea; 12th, "Polander Pete," boiler washer; 14th, I. N. "Nick" Wright, fireman; 15th, Silas Rapp, brakeman; 16th, Mr. Brady, Car Foreman; and 17th, Fireman Jack Shipard, who retired as an engineer. Mr. Shehea and Mr. Wright were the regular crew on Engine 505 at this time.   (Courtesy of Union Pacific Railroad)

OREGON SHORT LINE'S No. 618 came to grief in the coal fields of western Wyoming and Fred Jukes, venerable Western railroader-photographer, was on hand with his omnipresent camera to record the scene for posterity. The diamond stacked tenwheeler hit the snowy ground in the vicinity of the coal mines that burrowed into Wyoming's barren hills, overturning her tender in the process. The parent company of the Oregon Short Line had a finger in the coal mining pie, operating the Union Pacific Coal Company. Engine 618 of the Oregon Short Line was originally one of the road's 1400 series, built by the Rhode Island Locomotive Works in 1891; the Oregon Short Line & Utah Northern power was renumbered in 1897, at which time the 4-6-0 received the three-digit number shown on her tank. Her original specifications included 19½ x 24 inch cylinders, 51 inch drivers, and 170 pounds of working boiler pressure. The engine alone weighed 131,200 pounds. Note the canvas storm curtains at her gangways, hung there in a puny effort to help protect her engine crew from the icy winds that swept across the frozen plains when Winter's clutch grasped the arid wastes.

(Courtesy of Fred Jukes)

WESTWARD THE STEEL OF EMPIRE. A construction train on the Kansas Pacific Railway follows on the heels of tracklayers as the rails creep across the endless prairies. This scene, taken in the 1860's, shows the end of track some 300 miles west of the Missouri River. The Pacific Railroad Acts of 1862 and 1864 conferred a sizeable subsidy and land grant on the road, but by 1876 it was in receivership. Henry Villard, the German representing the foreign bondholders, was one of the Receivers appointed and his successful struggle with Jay Gould over Kansas Pacific policies laid the groundwork for his rise to fame with the Northern Pacific. The Kansas Pacific controlled the Denver Pacific Railway, the Denver & Boulder Valley Railway, the Arkansas Valley Railway, and the Junction City & Fort Kearney Railroad when the Receivers were appointed on November 3, 1876; the lines had 94 locomotives in service on a combined total of 914.6 miles of track, under the direction of Superintendent T. F. Oakes and Master of Machinery John McKenzie. Villard later brought Oakes to Oregon as an officer of the Oregon Railway & Navigation Co. and assisted him in his rise to power with the Northern Pacific.

(Courtesy of Union Pacific Railroad)

SNOW BLANKETS THE GROUND as a Union Pacific varnish blasts out of Rawlins, Wyoming, around 1907. The 1848, tossing her pillar of exhaust aloft in the chill air, was a 4-6-0 built by Baldwin in 1900, and the 8 cars of the westbound passenger made a hefty load for the old gal as she headed for Bitter Creek and Green River. This likeness of steam in action was recorded by that artist with a camera, Fred Jukes. The grand old railroader-photographer captured many similar views as he boomed around the American West and today his prints are a treasured possession, recalling an era when steam ruled the rails.

(Courtesy of Fred Jukes)

UNION PACIFIC RAILWAY, EASTERN DIVISION, started life as the Leavenworth, Pawnee & Western Railroad in 1861 and changed the name to Union Pacific Railway, Eastern Division, on June 6, 1863. Rogers Locomotive & Machine Works turned out the beautiful engine shown here in April, 1867. Named the SEMINOLE, the woodburning 4-4-0 measured 50 feet overall, weighed 115,000 pounds, and exerted 11,000 pounds tractive power. Her cab was a masterpiece of varnished walnut and ash; with ornate bell bracket, oil paintings on fluted sand dome and headlight, and a tasteful application of polished brass trimmings, the SEMINOLE was a delight to the eye. Her scrolled tender held 2,000 gallons of water and 2 cords of wood. An Act of Congress in 1869 changed the name of her road to the Kansas Pacific Railway; the line from Kansas City, Mo., to Denver, Colorado, was opened for service over it's 638 miles of main stem on September 1, 1870.
(Courtesy of Union Pacific Railroad)

SHOOTIN' NEWTON. Located north of the Arkansas River in Harvey County, Kansas, the old trail town of Newton was one of the boom villages that sprang into full flower as a shipping point for the countless numbers of long-horned cattle driven up the long trail from Texas. The riotous celebrations of the cowboys when they hit the rail shipping points were frequently punctuated by six-gun fire, and the Boot Hills of the trail towns were populated by victims of combat between the rowdy cattlemen and the forces of law and order. Occasionally railroad men were sent to Boot Hill too. An 0-4-0 switch engine is pictured here at the Santa Fe depot and yard office in Newton in 1871, when the great cattle drives were sending fleets of stock trains rolling over the Santa Fe rails
(Courtesy of Santa Fe Railway)

SANTA FE DEPOT at Topeka, Kansas, is shown here as it appeared around train time in 1880, with a wondrous variety of horse-drawn vehicles gathered near the station platform. In the early days, the railroad stations were the nerve centers of the community, the scene of the comings and goings of travellers and, via the railroad telegraph, the source of news from distant places. Election returns, the tidings of events, and the stories of disaster all came winging in on the chattering sounder. In small comunities, the citizenry often chipped in to provide a purse for a willing operator who would remain at his key after closing hours to bring them the latest news regarding some event of great interest. Before the advent of dining cars, many depots contained eating facilities for trainmen and passengers. Fred Harvey opened his first restaurant in the Topeka depot around 1875, and the high quality of food and service soon caused the famous Harvey Houses to be strung along the entire Santa Fe system. The Topeka "Dining Hall" sign and some of the white-clad attendants are visible over the box car at the far end of the depot. Harvey House girls were carefully chosen, the requisite being that they be of good character, attractive and intelligent. Many of them were wooed and won by the railroaders they served in the spotless Harvey dining rooms.

(Courtesy of Santa Fe Railway)

OLD KANSAS PACIFIC SWITCH ENGINE, No. 61 is shown here while working in the yards at Abilene, Kansas, in 1887. The little 0-4-0 was built by Hinkley & Williams around 1870 and had sloping cylinders and a four-wheel tender. Note the side-door caboose at right rear, with a single marker light mounted atop the cupola. The U.P. switchman perched on the pilot, at left, holds one of the old style coupling links, while the gent with the huge watch chain, standing on the footboard, holds a coupling pin; another pin is "cocked" in the forward three-slot draw-head, a method employed by trainmen to cut down the risk involved in making couplings. The link was guided into the slot and the jolt of the coupling would cause the "cocked" pin to fall into place, enabling the employee to hold the link with one hand and maintain a hold on the car or engine with the free member.

(Courtesy of Union Pacific Railroad)

BILENE KANS
1887

QUEEN OF THE COW TOWNS, the Babylon of the Plains, this 1873 photo shows Front Street in Dodge City, Kansas, looking east from Third Avenue. At left, the first false-front housed a harness shop and the second structure contained the United States Post Office; beyond the Plaza, to the right, can be seen the depot, windmill and water tank, and a locomotive of the Atchison, Topeka & Santa Fe Railroad. Dodge was noted for many things, but mostly for its wild and woolly ways. A shipping point for buffalo hides and bones, Texas cattle, and a jumping-off point for the frontier, it boasted of numerous saloons and gambling hells, plus a flourishing red light district. Thirsty cowboys, arriving in Dodge after a long dry drive up the trail, hurrahed the town and such noted peace officers as Wyatt Earp and Ed and Bat Masterson were hired to keep these wild characters under some semblance of control. The Santa Fe tracks ran down the middle of Front Street and the prudent crews doused their lanterns as they decorated the car tops into town after dark, for the lawless element took delight in demonstrating their skill with six-shooters, using the trainmen's lanterns for their targets. The saloons, dance halls, and gambling dens of Dodge were the scenes of many fatal shootings and the fame of its Boot Hill grew with the size of its silent population. (Courtesy of Santa Fe Railway)

MISSOURI MIX-UP occurred near Orrick, Missouri, on June 14, 1873. The Missouri, Kansas & Texas was ready to open their Tebo & Neosho Northeastern Extension between Sedalia and Moberly, but had no line running east out of Kansas City. The road dispatched a pair of Grant 4-4-0's from the terminal at Parsons, Kansas, via Fort Scott to Kansas City, where arrangements were made to run them over the road of the St. Louis, Kansas City & Northern to Moberly. Coupled ahead of Engine 30 of the StLKC&N, a Mason 4-4-0, the two Katy engines chuffed east. A rule in effect on the road at the time stated that if a train became more than 35 minutes late on its schedule, it was to proceed under flag protection and head in at the first opportunity and get new running orders. The triple-header became late but ignored or overlooked the fact and steamed blithely along toward Orrick, 32 miles east of Kansas City. In a tree-shaded stretch of woodland they met a west-bound freight and piled up in the jumble of motive power shown here. The westward freight was headed by Engine 72 of the St Louis, Kansas City & Northern, a 4-4-0 built by Rogers in 1870 for the predecessor North Missouri Railroad. It is reported that the StLKC&N engineer on the triple-header hit the ground running and never returned to the road.. His engine, No. 30 at far left, was a former St. Joseph & St. Louis Railroad locomotive, where she had been either No. 3, the L. M. LAWSON, or No. 4, the A. S. COUAR. (Courtesy of Dr. S. R. Wood)

MOTIVE POWER ON THE ATCHISON, TOPEKA & SANTA FE

Santa Fe's 738 was an odd type 4-4-2 with a Mother Hubbard cab and a secondary shelter at the rear for the fireman.
(Courtesy of Dr. S. R. Wood)

No. 625 was a Brooks 4-6-0 built in 1892, 18 x 24 inch cylinders and 63 inch drivers. Photo taken at the tank at Colorado Springs, Colorado, in 1898, showing the "butterfly" pilot plow.

No. 928 doubleheading out of Trinidad, Colorado, over Raton Pass. Baldwin's first tandem compound was a 2-10-0 built for the Santa Fe in 1902; in 1903 the Baldwin Works turned out a number of tandem compound 2-10-2's for the road and this wheel arrangement was named the Santa Fe type. Note the high and low pressure cylinders arranged in tandem fashion on both of these engines.
(Two photos, courtesy of Fred Jukes)

THE NORTH MISSOURI RAILROAD was incorporated in 1851 and built north and west from St. Louis through St. Charles, Mexico, Moberly, and other villages to Macon, Missouri, where the road connected with the pioneer Hannibal & St. Joseph Railroad. The North Missouri Railroad was reorganized in 1872 as the St. Louis, Kansas City & Northern, later a part of the Wabash system. The historic 4-4-0 shown here is the MINNESOTA, No. 19 of the old North Missouri Railroad. She was built by Swinburne, Smith & Company of Paterson, New Jersey, in 1852 and was the 49th locomotive constructed by this firm. Upon completion of the bridge over the Missouri River in 1856, the MINNESOTA was the first locomotive to cross and enter St. Charles, the historic Missouri outpost located on the peninsula between the Missouri and the Mississippi. The exploring party led by Lewis and Clark visited St. Charles on their way west in May, 1804, and were entertained by the French and Spanish inhabitants. Henry Clay French, the boomer railroader whose life has been so graphically recaptured in the book, "Railroadman," by his son, Chauncey Del French, was night telegrapher at St. Charles for the railroad in 1874.
(Courtesy of Dr. S. R. Wood)

IMPOSING WOODEN STATION of the St. Louis, Iron Mountain & Southern at Little Rock, Arkansas, is shown here as it appeared on June 14, 1890. The structure was built in 1872 by the old Cairo & Fulton Railroad, a line that was chartered in Missouri in 1851 and in Arkansas on January 12, 1853. The St. Louis & Iron Mountain Railroad, chartered in 1851, was opened for traffic in 1858. These roads, together with the Cairo, Arkansas & Texas, were consolidated on May 6, 1874, to form the St. Louis, Iron Mountain & Southern Railway, the latter concern eventually coming under the control of the Missouri Pacific. The Missouri Pacific demolished this ancient Little Rock station in October, 1909. The string of varnish shown here is Train 753, headed up by Engine 399. The cap-stacked 4-4-0 was built by Grant Locomotive Works in 1868 and was renumbered Missouri Pacific 8802 in December of 1905. Note the three-way stub switch in the left foreground.
(Courtesy of Dr. S. R. Wood)

MISSOURI PACIFIC SWITCH ENGINE 305 was typical of the yard engines in use in the West in the 1870-80 period. The little 0-6-0 was built by the Rogers Locomotive & Machine Works in Paterson, New Jersey for service on the Gould lines. Note the absence of running boards along her boiler and the one-lung air compressor mounted under the wooden cab. Her rear headlight is perched atop a metal frame to give it the necessary elevation, and an extension pipe mounted on her steam dome carried the escaping steam from her safety valve above the level of the cab roof. Sanders, manually operated by a rod from the cab, supply sand to the rail fore and aft of her main drivers for traction. (Courtesy of Fred Jukes)

MISSOURI PACIFIC RAILWAY was incorporated on October 21, 1876, taking over the foreclosed properties of the Pacific Railroad Company of Missouri. In 1880 a consolidation was effected which added the Lexington & St. Louis Railroad, Lexington & Southern Railroad, Kansas City & Eastern Railroad, St. Louis, Kansas & Arizona Railroad, Missouri River Railroad, Osage Valley & Southern Kansas Railroad, and the Leavenworth, Atchison & Northwestern Railroad to the Missouri Pacific lines. The line from St. Louis to a connection with Kansas Pacific was originally a broad gauge, 5 feet, 6 inches in width, but competition for the Western cattle traffic caused the road to convert to standard gauge. Section crews strung along the entire length of the road started work on Saturday, July 25, 1869, and in 16 hours they had shifted one rail toward the other over the whole road, creating a standard width of 4 feet, 8½ inches. Controlled for a time by the Atlantic & Pacific, the Missouri Pacific fell into the grasp of Jay Gould and formed the heart of his railroad empire, along with the St. Louis, Iron Mountain & Southern, Denver & Rio Grande, Wabash, Texas & Pacific, and such controlled lines as the Cotton Belt and the Katy. Shown here at Hermann, Missouri, in 1875 is Missouri Pacific's No. 152, a 2-6-0 built by Hinkley in 1870. (Courtesy of Dr. S. R. Wood)

BIG BRASS ON THE IRON MOUNTAIN.
A party of officials of the old St. Louis, Iron Mountain & Southern posed for this photograph near Granite Bend, Missouri, in 1912. On the ground are Finley J. Shepard, 1st Vice President E. J. Pierson, President B. F. Bush, two unidentified men, and, at the extreme right, John Cannon, Superintendent of the Iron Mountain at Poplar Bluff, Missouri. The derby-hatted gentleman at far left on the observation platform is C. L. Stone, Passenger Traffic Manager, and the smiling lady in black, right foreground, is Mrs. Finley J. Shepard, the former Helen Gould. The St. Louis, Iron Mountain & Southern Railway was long a Gould property; in earlier years George J. Gould was President, Frank Jay Gould, Vice President, and Howard Gould a member of the Board of Directors. The lines now form a part of the Missouri Pacific Railroad.
   (Courtesy of Missouri Pacific Railroad)

WABASH, ST. LOUIS & PACIFIC RAILWAY was formed in 1879 by a consolidation of the St. Louis, Kansas City & Northern Railway with the Wabash Railway, which had been operated as the Toledo, Wabash & Western Railroad until 1877. The St. Louis, Kansas City & Northern traced its ancestry back to the old North Missouri Railroad. The consolidation of 1879 was engineered by the Gould interests, and resulted in a main line extended from Toledo, Ohio, to Kansas City, via St. Louis, Missouri. Engine No. 345 of the Wabash, St. Louis & Pacific was a diamond stack 4-6-0 turned out for the road in 1880 by the Rhode Island Locomotive Works. Located in Providence, Rhode Island, this New England firm began turning out locomotives in 1866 and joined the combine to become part of the American Locomotive Works in 1901.

(Courtesy of Charles E. Fasher)

EARLY DAYS ALONG THE WABASH

WABASH, ST. LOUIS & PACIFIC RY. was formed in 1879 by a consolidation of the former Wabash Ry. (Toledo, Wabash & Western) and the St. Louis, Kansas City & Northern. The road emerged as the Wabash Western in 1887, with 640 miles of the system located west of the Mississippi, including lines to Des Moines, Omaha, and Kansas City. Engine 325, the COL. ROBT. ANDREWS, was built for the road in 1880 by Rogers. No. 1119 was a 4-4-0 from the Wabash Shops and No. 1351 was a 4-6-0 built by Rhode Island in 1880.

(Upper photo, courtesy of Wabash Railroad; Center and lower photos, courtesy of Chas. E. Fisher, Pres., R&LHS)

THE ROOTS OF THE ROCK ISLAND reach deeply into the historic past, the ancestral Rock Island & La Salle Railroad having been chartered in February, 1847. In 1851 the name was changed to Chicago & Rock Island Railroad, and this company was later consolidated with the Chicago, Rock Island & Pacific Railroad Company of Iowa. The rails had reached Rock Island in 1854, and by 1867 trains were running into Des Moines, Iowa. The westward extension to Council Bluffs was opened for traffic on June 8, 1869, creating a 500 mile rail route between Council Bluffs and Chicago. In June, 1880, the road was reorganized, absorbing a number of short lines and emerging as the Chicago, Rock Island & Pacific Railway. This photo shows Engine 222 of the new company, a 4-4-0 with the company's initials cast into the steam chest. Note the unusual caboose, a converted box car of the Chicago, Kansas & Nebraska Railroad, equipped with a locomotive headlight and a bench on the roof for the trainmen in lieu of the traditional cupola. Another item of interest is the mascot bird dog, seated on the water leg of the tank.   (Courtesy of the Chicago, Rock Island & Pacific Railroad)

FIRST CATTLE TRAIN from Caldwell, Kansas, to Chicago rolled over the Rock Island's rails on September 10, 1887. Hauled by Engine 97, a trim and speedy 4-4-0, the historic train is shown here with the crew posed for the photographer. Caldwell, located south of Wichita and near the border of Oklahoma Territory, enjoyed a lively career as a stock shipping center, with great herds of longhorns trailing up out of the plains of Texas and the Southwest for their train ride to the abattoir of the market centers. Tradition relates that the name of "cow-puncher" was hung onto the herdsmen who attended the cattle on these rail journeys by the railroaders; the stock train attendants carried prod poles to force fallen cattle onto their feet when the trains stopped, and it was this activity that led the "rails" to dub them "cow-punchers" or "cow-pokes."

(Courtesy of the Chicago, Rock Island & Pacific Railroad)

PRIDE OF THE ROCK ISLAND was the famous "Silver Engine," the AMERICA, one of the great locomotives that brought fame to American railroads and railroaders. The AMERICA was built by the Grant Locomotive Works in 1867, Shop No. 500, and was the showiest engine ever rolled of the Grant erecting floor. All of her fittings, trimmings, and the entire boiler jacket were of the finest quality German silver, and her cab was a masterpiece of the joiners' art, inlaid with select hardwood. She was shipped to the Universal Exposition in Paris, France, shortly after completion and won the highest awards and plaudits. Purchased by the Chicago, Rock Island & Pacific, she was given road number 109, retaining the name AMERICA. She opened the Rock Island service into Council Bluffs, Iowa, in May of 1869, took part in the great excursion over the Leavenworth line, and in 1871 she hung up some notable speed records in the Chicago-Omaha mail contract races, with a youth of 19 at her latch. This photo shows the dazzling beauty in her days of glory, silver jacket gleaming and a wealth of ornate scroll-work, oil painting on tender, and fancy castings on her cylinder saddle.

(Courtesy of Chicago, Rock Island & Pacific Railroad)

FIRST ENGINE ACROSS THE EADS BRIDGE was old No. 41 of the St. Louis, Vandalia & Terre Haute Railroad, a diamond stacked 4-4-0 that rolled across the completed structure at 4:40 P.M. on June 9th, 1874. Decorated for the occasion, she is shown here with her crew on the day she made the initial crossing; Engineer C. A. Sanborn is at the throttle, and Fireman J. A. Walker waves from the gangway. Fireman Walker was the owner of the original photograph of this scene, which was copied by that eminent railroad collector, Dr. S. R. Wood. The Eads Bridge, spanning the mighty Mississippi at St. Louis, was designed and supervised by Capt. James B. Eads, a civil engineer who later achieved fame for his system of jetties that cleared the mouth of the Mississippi and opened the noted South Pass channel. A later project of Eads that never materialized was a railway to transport ocean vessels across the Isthmus of Tehuantepec in Mexico. The great steel and stone arch bridge at St. Louis was formally dedicated for service at a "Grand Opening" held on July 4th, 1874, an event concluded with a monumental display of fireworks from the center span later in the evening. Hot weather during construction expanded some of the steelwork used in the bridge to such an extent that the parts would not fit, but this difficulty was overcome by packing the expanded parts with gunny sacks filled with ice, causing the metal to contract into the proper position.

(Courtesy of Dr. S. R. Wood)

ROCK ISLAND'S CAMELBACK No. 1889 posed for this shot near Horton, Kansas, with the engineer in the cab hung astraddle of the boiler and the fireman in the gangway beneath the scant shelter afforded him. The Camelback style of cab arrangement, such as applied to this compound Consolidation, was never very popular in the West. Horton, for many years called Horton Junction, was an important rail terminal on the Rock Island; the road split here, the southern line leading off to Topeka and the Southwest, while the north line led to Fairbury, Nebraska, before swinging back into Kansas on it's way west to Denver.

(Courtesy of
Chicago, Rock Island & Pacific Railroad)

DUBUQUE & SIOUX CITY RAILROAD was organized to take over the pioneer Dubuque & Pacific Railroad, which was sold under foreclosure on August 21, 1860. The former company had built 80 miles of road and the new management kept building west. The line was opened to Cedar Falls, Iowa, on April 1, 1861, giving the road its first 100 miles of track. Slowed by the Civil War, the rails reached the terminus at Iowa Falls in 1866. About this time the Dubuque & Sioux City leased the Cedar Falls & Minnesota Railroad, a struggling short line that had completed 14 miles of track from Cedar Falls to Waverly, Iowa. On September 13, 1867, the Dubuque & Sioux City leased their line and the Waverly road to the Illinois Central Railroad. The lines continued to operate under their original names; directors for the Dubuque & Sioux City in the late 1870's included James A. and Theodore Roosevelt and J. Pierpont Morgan. Under the Illinois Central lease, work was pushed on the branch north owned by the Cedar Falls & Minnesota, the line being open to the Minnesota State Line by 1870 and later reaching Albert Lea. Pictured here in the golden aura of yesteryear is the Illinois Central station at Ackley, Iowa, as it appeared on July 8, 1896. The horse-drawn omnibus and red order board suggests that the varnished cars may soon be due to clatter past the sun-drenched elevator and perhaps spot at the water tank while the wooden platform comes alive with the flurry of train-time activity. (Courtesy of Illinois Central Railroad)

ILLINOIS CENTRAL RAILROAD, primarily operating east of the Mississippi, acquired considerable trackage built by pioneer lines in Iowa. These included the Dubuque & Sioux City Railroad, Iowa Falls & Sioux City, and the Cedar Falls & Minnesota Railroad. The Dubuque & Sioux City was begun in 1856 as the Dubuque & Pacific Railroad; the first time table went into effect in May, 1857, and covered 29 miles of track from Dubuque to Dyersville. Early rules made conductors and engineers responsible for damages to equipment and provided that the cost of repairs would be deducted from their wages. Another rule read: "Being that the road is not fenced, and no cow-catchers, Engineers must keep a sharp lookout for cattle . . ." The Dubuque & Sioux City reached Cedar Falls in April, 1861, and was extended to Iowa Falls, 142 miles from Dubuque, in 1866; the road was leased to the Illinois Central in 1867. The Iowa Falls & Sioux City Railroad was opened between the points named in its title in 1870, a distance of 183.69 miles; the Cedar Falls & Minnesota Railroad completed 75 miles of track from Waterloo, Iowa, to the Minnesota State Line in 1870. Other roads acquired by the Illinois Central included the Cherokee & Dakota; Albert Lea & Southern; Staceyville Railroad; and the Fort Dodge & Omaha Railroad, the latter forming the main line from Tara to Council Bluffs. This view of Illinois Central's Engine 124 and her string of open-platform wooden cars is typical of passenger equipment used about 1887. Dubuque & Pacific engineers were cautioned: ". . . in no case run so as to risk the safety of the Train, the making of time now being only a secondary object. Let your motto be; 'Safe first and fast afterwards'." (Courtesy of Illinois Central Railroad)

THE FLAVOR OF WESTERN RAILROADING at the turn of the century is captured in this photo taken on the flat plains south of Cordell, Oklahoma, in 1904. The ten-wheeler boiling along with her nine cars and a caboose is No. 411 of the Frisco, a Rogers product of 1880 that was formerly SLSF No. 161. Although the engine is equipped with air brake equipment, the brakemen decorating the car tops calls up memories of a decade or two earlier, when only hand brakes were in use and the trainmen spent most of their time on the swaying running boards, manning the brake staffs to help control the speed of the train. In 1907, the engine shown here plunged into the Cimarron River; she was fished out and placed back in service, but her tender was lost and never recovered. (Courtesy of collection of Dr. S. R. Wood)

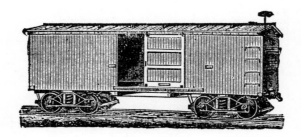

South by Southwest.

The focal point for railroad operations along the lower reaches of the Mississippi was the ancient city of New Orleans, historic port located above the head of the great delta at the mouth of the Father of Waters. Known as the Crescent City, the town of New Orleans laid claim to one of the earliest railway operations in the United States. In 1831 a privately-owned tram road, five miles in length and operated by horsepower, was placed in operation between New Orleans and Lake Ponchartrain, offering passenger service to the venturesome. A steam locomotive was placed in service on this road in 1832, one of the earliest of its kind to operate in this country.

MORGAN'S LOUISIANA & TEXAS No. 9 had formerly carried the same number on the New Orleans, Opelousas & Greeat Western Railroad. Built by Taunton in 1857, she had 63 inch drivers, 14 x 22 inch cylinders, and weighed 62 000 pounds. This photo shows her at the Algiers terminal and was probably taken in July, 1884; the slatted wooden building at left is the old California shed, while the brick building at right is the old New York shed. Engineer John Graham is seated in the ornately-panelled cab and Fireman W. T. Donner stands in the gangway; Steve Spahr stands on the pilot beam and Switchman Sullivan is on the ground by the pilot, while Switchman Goodwine stands beside the tank. In 1886 this engine became Southern Pacific No. 509, but had vanished from the roster by 1901.

(H. J. Heaney collection, courtesy of Texas & New Orleans Railroad)

The Pontchartrain Railroad and the Jefferson & Lake Pontchartrain both linked New Orleans with Lake Pontchartrain, and the Mexican Gulf Railroad meandered southeasterly from the Crescent City of Proctorville.

Railroad building in the area languished until 1851, when a group of prominent Louisiana men revived the dream of a rail line reaching west into Texas, with the visionaries among them predicting the steel would span the Southwest and terminate on the shores of the Pacific Ocean. The Opelousas, Attakapas & New Orleans Railroad was organized in 1851 and some survey lines were run. After the great Southern & Western Railroad Convention was held in January, 1852, state laws were changed to encourage railroad construction and the Attakapas project was reorganized as the New Orleans, Opelousas & Great Western Railroad.

One of the most prominent figures connected with this pioneer road was Mr. G. W. R. Bayley, who directed much of the original location and served as Chief Engineer from 1855 until 1869. The road had its eastern terminus at Algiers, across the Mississippi from New Orleans, and ran west to Des Allemands, thence across the vast boggy region known as the Trembling Prairies to Bayou Lafourche. West of that waterway, the line crossed Devil's Swamp, Chacahoula Swamp, and Tiger Swamp. These cypress swamps and the Trembling Prairies offered some of the most difficult railroad construction ever encountered, The Trembling Prairie was a crust of earth floating on water five to ten feet deep, necessitating endless piling

trestles, fills, and cribwork. The swamps and the "prairies tremblante were alive with snakes, alligators, and mosquitoes, and outbreaks of yellow fever decimated the construction gangs and officials with great impartiality. Men worked in water waist-deep to hack their way through the dense growths of cypress, hampered by heavy rains and high waters. Crevasses in the great levee along the Mississippi flooded the region, damaging the roadbed and halting all work for a time.

In spite of these great difficulties, work was pushed on the road and the officers had set a date in March, 1853, for the opening of the first section, but once again Fate took a hand and blasted the plans of the railroaders.

The New Orleans, Opelousas and Great Western had sent Director Ambrose Lanfear and Bernard Fallon to the East in early 1853 to purchase locomotives and rolling stock, then on to England to purchase 40 miles of rail. The first locomotive ordered was a 4-4-0 weighing 20 tons. The engine was built by M. W. Baldwin in 1853 and bore his factory number 512; her specifications included $13\frac{1}{2}$ x 24 inch cylinders and 60 inch drivers, and she cost the Louisiana road $6,000.

Named the OPELOUSAS and bearing No. 1, the pioneer engine was shipped aboard the brig, CIMBRUS, and was scheduled to arrive at Algiers in March, 1853. Misfortune overtook the CIMBRUS, however, and she and her precious cargo went to the bottom near Key West, Florida. In May of 1853, wreckers succeeded in raising the locomotive from the sunken brig and it was fired up and found to be in working order. The underwriters ordered her returned to the factory, however, and she was not delivered at Algiers until September of 1853. Safely landed, the OPELOUSAS was promptly put to work hauling material trains for the contractors engaged in building the road.

On November 1, 1853, the road received two 4-4-0 type engines built by Niles & Company of Cincinnati, Ohio. These locomotives weighed 18 tons each, and became No. 2, the NATCHITOCHES, and No. 3, the TEXAS; their cost was $7,250 each. The fourth engine for the line, another 4-4-0, was delivered in December of 1853. Built by Rogers, Ketchum & Grosvenor of Paterson, New Jersey, she bore Shop No. 421 and cost $8,357.75. This engine was named the CHRISTOPHER ADAMS, JR., in honor of the first president of the road. She was the largest engine yet acquired, weighing 24 tons, and had 12½ x 22 inch cylinders and 72 inch drivers. The officials thought her too large and too fast for the newly-laid track and she spent much of her time in reserve.

The first passenger train over the New Orleans, Opelousas & Great Western was an excursion operated on December 3, 1853. The engine, NATCHITOCHES, shoved two passenger cars and a number of platform cars fitted with seats out to a point known as St. Charles, where refreshments and oratory were served up to the invited guests. On the return trip to Algiers the engineer opened the latch on the NATCHITOCHES and covered the 17 miles in 24 minutes, the Niles & Co. eightwheeler being clocked at 55 miles per hour over a portion of the run. Regular passenger service to Boutte, 24 miles west of Algiers, was placed in operation before the end of the year.

On June 18, 1854, the rails of the new road reached Bayou Des Allemands, 32 miles west of Algiers, and crossed the swampy "prairies tremblante" to reach Bayou Lafourche on November 6, 1854. Two new locomotives were added to the roster in 1854, the first being a 17 ton 4-4-0 built by Rogers, Ketchum & Grosvenor, Shop No. 451. This engine was used for passenger service, was assigned road number 5, and bore the name GREAT WESTERN. She was delivered in February and in April the road received Engine 6, the LOUISIANA. This 4-4-0 was built by Anderson & Co., probably in what was the Tredegar Works in Richmond, Virginia. She weighed 25 tons and proved to be too heavy for the light track, so spent much of her time stationed at Bayou Lafourche as a relief engine.

The Opelousas in the corporate title of the road caused the local wits to dub the line "Applesauce," but business was flourishing and the volume of traffic over the road was sending a steady flow of cash into the company coffers. When the road reached Bayou Lafourche, it became necessary to construct a drawbridge in order to allow the bayou steamboats freedom of passage. This draw span, or spans, was designed by Chief Engineer G. W. R. Bayley and was unique enough to merit a brief description. The bridge consisted of two separate draw sections, with iron rails mounted on their under sides; these rails passed over heavy iron wheels mounted atop the bridge piers. The shorter section was rolled to one side to a set of piers, and could be moved by two men. The main draw section was then pulled back across the regular piers to the position formerly occupied by the smaller span, this movement being activated by a span of mules operating a windlass. When the short span was rolled aside and the main span hauled toward shore, a channel 71 feet wide was created, providing ample room

RARE VIEW OF CIVIL WAR VINTAGE, this photograph was taken about 1865 and shows the Algiers, Louisiana, depot of the New Orleans, Opelousas & Great Western Railroad. At the left, heading a freight train, stands NOO&GW Eng. 4, named the CHRISTOPHER ADAMS, JR., in honor of the road's first president. This 4-4-0 was built by Rogers, Ketchum & Grosvenor in 1853, had 12½ x 22 inch cylinders, 72 inch drivers, and weighed 24 tons; she later became No. 15 on the roster of the Morgan's Louisiana & Texas. Coupled to the coach at right is a 4-4-0 bearing the lettering of the United States Military Railroad. During the Yankee occupation of Louisiana, the NOO&GW was under Federal control and two locomotives were built by the Union railroads in the Algiers shops; these engines were named the W. G. HEWES and the COL. HOLABIRD, and one of them may be the locomotive pictured here at the right. Military Railroad records indicate that at one time during the Civil War, the CHRISTOPHER ADAMS was in use on the Memphis & Little Rock Railroad, under Federal control. (G. M. Best collection, courtesy of Texas & New Orleans Railroad)

FAMILIAR STAR EMBLEM on smokebox number plate serves to identify this cap-stacked 4-4-0 as a Morgan line engine. Built by Baldwin around 1883, she was Morgan's Louisiana & Texas No. 47, the last engine acquired by the ML&T before that road was taken over by the Southern Pacific. A classic example of the American Standard type, this locomotive was displayed at the New Orleans Exposition of 1884-85, and is shown here with a group of railroaders while coupled to the business car, MORGAN. Renumbered 547 and later 127, the engine was scrapped in 1912. Men in right background are standing on stock cars belonging to the Galveston, Harrisburg & San Antonio Railway.

for the passage of the steamboats plying Bayou Lafourche. On the shore opposite the moving draw sections, a third fixed span carried the rails out to connect with the moveable portion of Bayley's structure.

Completed in 1855, this bridge served until it was replaced with a more conventional swinging drawbridge in 1860. This span was destroyed in 1862 by rebel raiders.

Prior to the outbreak of the Civil War, the railroad had been enjoying a prosperous trade, with herds of Texas cattle arriving by steamer from various Gulf ports to the rail terminus at Bayou Boeuf and later at the new western end of track at Brashear City (now Morgan City). Sidewheel steamers brought the longhorns from such Gulf shipping points as Galveston and Matagorda Bay, the first boat lines being operated by Commodore Cornelius Vanderbilt and later these were acquired by purchase by Charles Morgan.

The great crevasse in the levee along the Mississippi that broke through on Bell's plantation in April 11, 1858, flooded the railroad for six months, causing the management to later raise the embankments of the grade to prevent future repetitions.

Louisiana seceded from the Union in January of 1861 and the New Orleans, Opelousas & Great Western embraced the rebel cause, furnishing free transportation to the Confederate forces. The city of New Orleans was captured in April, 1862, and the railroad was taken over by troops of the 21st Indiana Regiment, Colonel J. McMillan commanding.

The ensuing war years brought trouble and exciting adventure to the line. When the Yankee bluecoats took over, the civilian locomotive engineers and other employees refused to work the road and the Union officers replaced them with new men, many of them proving to be incompetent railroaders. Wrecks took place and

locomotives were damaged, reducing the efficiency of the line.

The infamous Major General Benjamin F. Butler, Union commander of the area and a man deeply hated by Louisiana residents, ordered the road returned to the owners in May of 1862, and demanded that operations be resumed to supply food to the city of New Orleans. Thus far, the struggle for control of the railroad had all proved favorable to the Union captors, but there was still fight left in the Southern forces. On May 26th the commander of the 9th Brigade of Louisiana Militia dispatched a company of Confederate Rangers from St. Martinsville in a foray against the rail line. These raiders captured a train at Bayou Boeuf and ran down the line to Jefferson Station, near Avondale, practically under the noses of the Yankee troops quartered in Algiers and New Orleans. These daring invaders, in a coup more highly successful than the much-publicized Andrews' raid, proceeded to tear up the track and then withdrew to Berwick's Bay, burning the bridges at Des Allemands, Lafourche, and Bayou Boeuf as they went. This coup left the road divided, the Confederates retaining three locomotives and about half of the road's rolling stock on the western section.

In July of 1862 the eastern end of the line was returned to Union Army operations, headed by Colonel S. Thomas of the 8th Vermont Regiment. The Federal troops operated the 32 mile section from Algiers to the burned bridge at Des Allemands and the rebel forces used the western end of the road. This situation existed until November of 1862, when the Yankees pulled a surprise raid. Mounting cannons on flat cars and using temporary bridges to span the bayous, the Union troops rolled west, capturing the entire 80 miles of track to Berwick's Bay. As this rail-borne Juggernaut advanced, the Confederates fought a rear guard action and were able to destroy two locomotives, along with buildings and considerable rolling stock. Another serious blow to the road was the loss of the sidewheeler CERES, the ferry boat plying between New Orleans and the Algiers railhead. The CERES, pressed into service as a Union transport, was blown up at Ship Island in October of 1862. The railroad had purchased the vessel in 1860 to replace the steamboat B. E. CLARK, a previous ferry purchased in 1857 and destroyed by fire in 1860.

With the railroad in Union hands, military operations were resumed, but the rebels still managed to get in an occasional blow at the invaders. Late in 1863 the Federal troops of the 97th Illinois Volunteers arrived at Brashear City after a march across Louisiana, and were entrained for Algiers. A mixed troop and freight train departed for Algiers, followed by a troop train loaded with the Illinois Volunteers. It was a dark night as the two trains chuffed along, sparks from their wood fires erupting from the funnel stacks. The leading train's locomotive was in charge of a civilian engineer, a native railroader hostile to the Yankee invaders. Seizing an opportunity to inflict a blow on the occupying Northerners, this runner stopped his train in a timbered section of the dark and dismal swamplands and escaped into the woods. No lights or protection were provided to the rear of the stalled train and the second section soon came boiling along through the night and ploughed into the standing train with a resounding crash. When the wreckage was cleared away, 13 Union men lay dead and 66 more were seriously injured. The first section had included several cars loaded with sugar and the surviving Yankee troopers, starved for sweets, gorged themselves on the contents of the damaged cars. The over-indulgence purged the men violently, rendering many of them incapable of duty for several days.

In February, 1866, the Federal Government returned the sorry remains of the road to its owners. Under the military control, two of the locomotives had been shipped north to the Memphis & Little Rock Railroad and a third engine sent to the Brazos, Santiago & Brownsville Railroad; these engines were never returned. The nine engines remaining on the road were in poor repair, and out of 230 freight and passenger cars the road got back only 45 damaged freight cars and some parts of wrecked rolling stock. In addition, the drawbridges were destroyed and these had to be rebuilt. The gross revenues for 1860 had amounted to over $481,-000, yet the directors found only $129.38 in the treasury when they took the road back in 1866.

Pressed for finances, the road tried hard for a comeback, but the hard times following the Civil War in the South finally caused the line to be sold at a sheriff's public auction. The new owner of the New Orleans, Opelousas & Great Western was Charles Morgan, operator of the first steamships on the Gulf of Mexico. Morgan purchased the railroad in May, 1869, and renamed it Morgan's Louisiana & Texas Railroad.

One of Morgan's important actions was changing the road from broad to standard gauge in July, 1872. He also inaugurated the car ferry system across the Mississippi, abolishing the old method requiring the trans-shipment of all freight.

In 1871, after failing to extend the railroad west, Morgan sold the grade and franchises west of Berwick's Bay to the New Orleans, Mobile & Texas Railroad. This outfit did some grading but abandoned the extension in 1872. The holdings of this company were bought back by the Morgan's Louisiana & Texas Railroad and Steamship Company, a corporation Morgan formed shortly before he died on May 8, 1878.

Charles Morgan earned the respect of his railroaders. He insisted that they be paid adequate wages regularly in a time when many roads often allowed the payrolls to fall far in arrears. So pleasant and punctual was the arrival of the ML&T pay car that even today rail-

ATLANTIC SYSTEM ENGINE 111 of the Southern Pacific was a 4-4-0 built by Baldwin in 1879 as No. 24 of the old Morgan's Louisiana & Texas. In 1885 she was renumbered 524, and in 1901 became the 111. This photo of the three-domed American type was taken at Algiers, Louisiana, in 1913, shortly before the engine was scrapped.
(H. J. Heaney collection, courtesy of Texas & New Orleans Railroad)

roaders in the region use the expression, "regular as payday on the Morgan." In 1876, the citizens of Brashear City renamed their town Morgan City in honor of this considerate railroad operator.

After Morgan's death, construction work pushed the rails west, the track reaching Vermilionville in March of 1880. Berwick's Bay bridge was completed in 1881, one of the most noted structures in the South, having a length of 1,835 feet. The line from Vermilionville (renamed Lafayette in 1884) was extended to Cheneyville in 1882, where a connection was made with the Texas & Pacific.

In 1878 the Louisiana Western Railroad built from Vermilionville to the Sabine River. On the Texas side of this stream, a sister corporation called the Louisiana Western Extension completed six and one half miles of track to a connection with the old Texas & New Orleans Railroad at Orange, Texas. The latter road ran from Houston to Orange, about 105 miles. With the completion of the Sabine River bridge, New Orleans had a direct rail route to Houston, Texas. These lines were later gathered into the fold of the Southern Pacific, forming that road's present Texas & New Orleans, the so-called Atlantic System.

Backtracking a bit, the reader may be interested to learn of some of the early short lines operated in Louisiana, a few of which were mentioned at the start of this chapter.

The Pontchartrain Railroad, incorporated in 1830, was a standard gauge line 4½ miles long running from New Orleans to Milnesburg. The line was completed in 1831 and horses were first used. The first locomotive was placed in service in 1832. An engine built by John Shields of Cincinnati proved a failure but was used as a stationary engine. The PONTCHARTRAIN, a 2-2-0 type built in 1832 by Rothwell was next on the roster, followed by the CREOLE, an 0-4-0 built by Bury in 1834. This engine was followed by the FULTON, built by Hicks in 1834 and by the ORLEANS, an 0-4-0 built by Bury in 1836. This historic road was acquired by the Louisville & Nashville and was abandoned in 1932.

The New Orleans & Carrollton Railroad began operations with horses over 7¼ miles of track in 1835. The road was broad gauge, 5 feet 6 inches in width. The first locomotives used were a pair of 4-2-0's built by Norris in 1836. Named the INDUSTRY and the ENTERPRISE, these engines had 48 inch drivers and 10½ x 18 inch cylinders. In 1837 the road received two more Norris 4-2-0 types, the LAFAYETTE and the WASHINGTON. The fifth engine, NEW ORLEANS, was built by Hicks in 1838. This line was finally converted to electricity in 1893.

The Mexican Gulf Railroad was incorporated in 1837 and built a strap iron road from New Orleans to Lake Borgne, 5 miles. Failing shortly after completion, it was taken over and operated by the State of Louisiana. The first engine, named the LAKE BORGNE, was a 4-2-0 built by Norris in 1837, followed by a second Norris engine of the same type built in 1838. This engine bore the name NEW ORLEANS.

Upstream from New Orleans, the Clinton & Port Hudson Railroad completed 28 miles of track in 1839, the road having been organized in 1833. This was one of the first roads in Louisi-

HOUSTON & TEXAS CENTRAL RAILWAY was originally incorporated in 1848 as the Galveston & Red River, the change of names taking place in 1865. Construction started at Houston on a line projected to Dallas, but the Civil War halted the work near Millican until 1867. The acquisition of short lines, such as the Ft. Worth & New Orleans, eventually led to a system extending from Houston to Ft. Worth and Dallas and Austin to Hempstead. The road became part of the Southern Pacific lines in 1921. Engine 70 of the Houston & Texas Central was an 0-4-0 named the BISON. She was built by the Dickson Locomotive Works of Scranton, Pennsylvania, in 1876 and bore Shop No. 197. Note the extreme height of the footboards above the rail, a feature later changed in the interests of safety for the life and limbs of switchmen.

(Courtesy of Texas & New Orleans Railroad)

ana to use Baldwin locomotives, the CLINTON, a 4-2-0 of 1836 vintage being Matt Baldwin's 52nd engine. The line also used the engines PORT HUDSON and JACKSON, Baldwin 4-2-0's built in 1838 and 1839. The Civil War must have wrought havoc with the road's motive power, for it was operated by horsepower from 1865 until around 1875 when a steam locomotive was acquired.

In central Louisiana, the Alexandria & Cheneyville completed 20 miles of track from Alexandria, on the Red River, to Cheneyville. This concern was incorporated in 1837 and had completed 6 miles of track by 1839, using two locomotives.

Up the Mississippi from Port Hudson, the little West Feliciana Railroad was placed in operation in 1835. This road ran from St. Francisville, Louisiana, on the famed Bayou Sara, to Woodville, Mississippi, a distance of 28 miles. The road used some early Baldwin 4-2-0 types, the WOODVILLE being Baldwin's 43rd engine, built in 1836, and the FELICIANA was a Baldwin product of 1839.

Other early Louisiana railways included the Baton Rouge, Grosse Tete & Opelousas Railroad, a broad gauge (5 feet 6 inches) line operated from a point opposite Baton Rouge west to Lombard, Louisiana, 28 miles, in operation at the start of the Civil War, and the Vicksburg, Shreveport & Texas Railroad. This latter line was also of 5 foot 6 inch gauge, and extended for 72 miles from Delta, opposite Vicksburg, west to Monroe, Louisiana. The road was reorganized in the 1870's as the North Louisiana & Texas Railroad, but reverted back to the former title with a minor change, becoming the Vicksburg, Shreveport & Pacific Railroad. In 1901 this road was reorganized, emerging as the Vicksburg, Shreveport & Pacific Railway, controlled by the Alabama, New Orleans, Texas & Pacific Junction Railways Company, Ltd., an English group formed in London around 1881. The road from Delta to Monroe had been so hard hit by Union raiders during the Civil War that it had been forced to cease operations, but the line was later extended west to Shreveport, 171 miles west of Delta. This road later passed into the hands of the Illinois Central and the 17 mile westward extension from Shreveport to Waskom, Texas, became a part of the Missouri, Kansas & Texas.

Railroad fever got an early grip on Texans, with a charter for a line being granted by the First Congress of the Republic of Texas in 1836, the first charter granted for a railway west of

HOUSTON & TEXAS CENTRAL RAILROAD was organized August 1, 1889, as the successor to the Houston & Texas Central Railway. In 1901 the new company absorbed the Austin & Northwestern Railroad, the Fort Worth & New Orleans Railway, and the Central Texas & Northwestern Railway. A 23 mile extension from Burnet to Lampasas was opened in 1902, branching north from the line between Austin and Llano, Texas. Another short branch off the Austin-Llano line extended about 7 miles south from Fairland to Marble Falls. Fort Worth was reached by the branch running northwesterly off the main line at Garret. The Austin branch between Hempstead and Brenham, opened in 1866, was built under the charter of the Washington County Railroad, and the Houston & Texas Central completed the road into Austin in 1871. The road was originally built to a gauge of 5 feet 6 inches, but was changed to standard gauge in the mid-1870's. The Texas Legislature made a grant to the line of 16 sections for every mile constructed and equipped. The 4-6-0- shown here was originally No. 127, built by Cooke in 1892 under Shop No. 2210. She was renumbered 327 and finally scrapped in 1937. Her oil headlight has been converted to electricity, the dynamo mounted on the boiler between the stack and the bell.

(Courtesy of Fred Jukes)

"HELL EITHER WAY YOU TAKE IT" was the monicker applied by wags to the Houston, East & West Texas Railway. In the early 1870's, the Shreveport, Southwestern & Rio Grande Consolidated Railroad planned a narrow gauge line from Shreveport to the Rio Grande and some construction was undertaken. The Houston, East & West Texas was incorporated in 1875 and completed 191 miles of 3 foot gauge road from Houston, Texas, to Logansport, Louisiana. At the latter terminus on the banks of the Sabine River, connections were made with the 3 foot gauge Shreveport & Houston Railway, extending 40 miles east to Shreveport. The Southern Pacific Railway acquired control of these lines in 1893 and the roads were broadened to standard gauge in 1895. The roads were operated in connection with the Houston & Texas Central, forming what was known as the Central Lines, until consolidated with the S.P. in 1912. Engine 31 of the Houston, East & West Texas Railway was a neat 4-6-0, Baldwin built in 1898, the same year that the roaming camera of Fred Jukes caught her in this pose at Shreveport, Louisiana. The eagle-eye is giving her the once-over while the fireboy watches from the gangway; note the wood piled on her tank, ready for consumption in her roaring firebox.   (Courtesy of Fred Jukes)

the Mississippi. The Harrisburg & Brazos Railroad did some grading in 1840, but the project failed and the first successful operating road was the Buffalo Bayou, Brazos & Colorado Railway, chartered in 1850.

Construction on the Buffalo Bayou line started at Harrisburg in 1851 and the first locomotive, GENERAL SHERMAN, was placed in service late in 1852. This locomotive, named in honor of General Sidney Sherman, hero of the battle of San Jacinto, was a 4-2-0 type built by Baldwin; she was inside connected and weighed 13 tons. Engineer F. A. Stearns wheeled her over the first 20 miles of track in August, 1853, on an excursion to Stafford's Point; mounted on flat cars were two cannon loaned by General Sam Houston to help celebrate the completion of the first section of the road.

By 1861, the Buffalo Bayou, Brazos & Colorado had completed 80 miles of track, reaching Alleyton on the Colorado River. Included in this road was a low bridge with a pontoon center section over the Brazos River; steep inclines led down both banks to this structure, making it necessary for the trains to dash across it at high speed in order to climb the opposite bank. Passengers were given the privilege of walking across the span, if they did not wish to risk the wild ride over the shaky structure. The road

acquired an 0-4-0 built by Seth Wilmarth in 1856, and this engine was named the TEXAS; later the line purchased some 4-4-0's, including the AUSTIN, COLUMBUS, RICHMOND, and HARRISBURG.

The Civil War left the line in poor condition, its equipment battered and the treasury insolvent. In 1870 the Buffalo Bayou, Brazos & Colorado was reorganized as the Galveston, Harrisburg & San Antonio Railway; with funds advanced by Boston merchant Thos. W. Peirce, the road was extended to San Antonio in 1877 and in 1883 the westering line connected with the Southern Pacific at a point two and one half miles west of the old Pecos River Bridge, forming part of the southern transcontinental route.

From such humble beginnings, the numerous rail lines of the Southwest grew into major systems. They hauled the cotton and cattle to market, and their wooden coaches drove the horse-drawn stage lines into oblivion. The individual stories of the many various companies that rose and fell are too lengthy to include here, but the part these roads played in building the great Southwest Empire was a vital one and the existing lines are a living tribute to the courage of the men who brought the iron harbingers of civilization into the sprawling region.

GALVESTON, HARRISBURG & SAN ANTONIO Engine 748 was a cap-stacked 4-4-0 built by Schenectady in 1892 and later renumbered Southern Pacific 231 before being scrapped in 1931. When the famous old "Sunset Limited" was placed in service, this American Standard coal burner handled the run between El Paso and Sanderson, Texas. (Courtesy of Texas & New Orleans Railroad)

GALVESTON, HARRISBURG & SAN ANTONIO RAILWAY was formed in 1870 to take over the former Buffalo Bayou, Brazos & Colorado Railway. The new organization extended the line from Alleyton to San Antonio, Texas, and through service from Harrisburg to San Antonio was inaugurated on March 1, 1877, with construction in progress on an extension two miles beyond San Antonio to the cattle yards. The line later became a part of the Southern Pacific's Texas & New Orleans holdings. Engine 28, the MARION WENTWORTH, was built by Hinkley in 1876, Shop No. 1235; a dressy 4-4-0, she had 16 x 24 inch cylinders and 56 inch drivers. At one time in her career, she served on the Gulf, Western Texas & Pacific, a road incorporated in 1871 to take over the San Antonio & Mexican Gulf Roalroad; this latter road was one of the early Texas lines, built between Indianola and Port Lavaca via Victoria. The Civil War played havoc with this 5½ foot gauge road and in post-war years it was rebuilt and the successor Gulf, Western Texas & Pacific extended it to Cuero in 1873. The road was taken over by the Galveston, Harrisburg & San Antonio in 1885. (Courtesy of Chas. E. Fisher)

AMERICAN STANDARD BY ROGERS, this shot of Engine 18 of the Houston, East & West Texas Railway was taken by the veteran Fred Jukes at Shreveport, Louisiana, in 1898. There is no record of a name applied to Engine 18, the woodburner shown here, but earlier locomotives on the road and the closely-related Shreveport & Houston had carried such names as NACOGDOCHES, SHEPHERD, LUFKIN, SHREVEPORT, T. W. HOUSE, S. C. TIMPSON, and KEATCHIE. (Courtesy of Fred Jukes)

SAN ANTONIO & ARANSAS PASS RAILWAY was incorporated in 1884 and built 238 miles of standard gauge line from Houston to San Antonio, Texas. A 70-mile extension from San Antonio carried the road northwest to Kerrville, and branches were built from Yoakum to Waco, Kenedy to Corpus Christi, Gregory to Rockport, Skidmore to Falfurrias, and Austin Junction to Lockhart. The road was reorganized in 1893 and operated as an affiliate of the Southern Pacific until 1925, when it was absorbed by that system. In 1905 the San Antonio & Aransas Pass was operating about 724 miles of road, and was known as "The Mission Route"; colorful passes issued in the 1890's showed Missions San Jose and Concepcion and bore the bold and flourishing signature of General Manager W. D. Monserrati. In later years the Southern Pacific extended the line from Falfurrias south through Hidalgo County to a point near Edinburg, where the road veered east and south through Harlingen to a terminus at Brownsville, Texas, near the mouth of the Rio Grande. This photo shows Engine 23, formerly named the W. H. MAVERICK, with a short passenger train posed on a bridge. The 4-4-0 was built by Baldwin in 1887, Shop No 8745, and was later renumbered 35, but was gone from the San Antonio & Aransas Pass at the time of the consolidation with the Southern Pacific in 1925. The S. A. & A. P. lines were incorporated into the Victoria Division of the Texas & New Orleans, the Atlantic System of the Southern Pacific.

(Collection of Dr. S. R. Wood)

TYLER TAP RAILROAD, a narrow gauge Texas short line slightly over 22 miles long, was the ancestor of the Cotton Belt Route. Organized by Major James P. Douglas, a former Confederate artillery officer, and other local citizens, the Tyler Tap was chartered in 1871 and grading started in 1875. By 1877 the line was in operation from Tyler to Sandy Switch, using a locomotive named the GOVERNOR HUBBARD. Financial problems beset the road and President Douglas interested the owners of the St. Louis Cotton Compress Company in its possibilities. In 1879 the Texas & St. Louis Railway was organized by these financiers to take over the Tyler Tap and extend it west to Waco, Texas, and east to a junction with the Iron Mountain line at Texarkana. One of the early locomotives on the Texas & St. Louis was No. 3, the M. C. HUMPHREY. The 2-6-0 was built by Brooks in February, 1880, and bore Shop No. 375. Pot on cab roof was part of the vacuum brake equipment.

(Collection of Dr. S. R. Wood)

Texas & St. Louis Railway's No. 5 was a Brooks 4-4-0 named the J. W. PARAMORE, built in 1879 under Shop No. 345. She was named in honor of Col. James W. Paramore, Yankee army officer who became president of the road from 1880 to 1885.
(Collection of Dr. S. R. Wood)

Texas & St. Louis No. 46 was named the THOS. E. TUTT. She was built by Grant in 1882 and was a woodburner; the Cotton Belt inaugurated oil for fuel in 1898, the first Southwest road to do so.

(Collection of Dr. S. R. Wood)

Texas & St. Louis 51 was a 4-4-0 built by Grant in 1882 and named the A. W. SOPER. The 3-foot gauge woodburner was converted to standard gauge in the Tyler, Texas, shops in 1889. (Courtesy of St. Louis Southwestern Railway)

TEXAS & ST. LOUIS RAILWAY, after having absorbed the old Tyler Tap Railroad, commenced construction of a 3-foot gauge road east to the Mississippi River. Jay Gould had obtained control of the St. Louis, Iron Mountain & Southern, hence the decision of the Texas & St. Louis to extend their line east of the original proposed connection with the Iron Mountain at Texarkana. In late 1881, they consolidated with the slim-gauge Little River Valley & Arkansas Railroad, a short line running through the Nigger Wool Swamp region of Missouri from Malden to New Madrid. About 6 miles west of New Madrid, the T. & St. L. built a branch from the former Little River Valley & Arkansas Railroad to Bird's Point, Missouri, where trains could be ferried across the Mississippi to Cairo, Illinois, and a connection with the Illinois Central. By 1883, the Texas & St. Louis was in operation from Bird's Point, Mo., to Gatesville, Texas, via Paragould and Pine Bluff, Arkansas. On October 19, 1882, the road purchased a Mogul from the Grant Loco. Works that became No. 56, the O B. FILLEY. The woodburner is depicted here in a view copied from a faded photograph; note the swampy timberland and the bales of cotton on the wooden platform ahead of the engine.   (Courtesy of St. Louis Southwestern Railway)

A SILVER SPIKE was pounded home on the newly-constructed bridge over the Arkansas River at Rob Roy, Arkansas, in 1883, linking the final segments of the Texas & St. Louis Ra lway from Bird's Point, Missouri, to Gatesville, Texas. Typical freight power on the road at that time was Engine 84, the JOHN KRAUSS, a narrow gauge 2-6-0 woodburner shown here as she appeared in 1884. This Mogul was converted to standard gauge in 1887. Floods, strikes, and lack of equipment forced the Texas & St. Louis Ry. into receivership early in 1884 and the St. Louis, Arkansas & Texas Railway was formed to acquire the old "Cotton Belt Route" in 1886. The lines in Missouri and Arkansas were changed to standard gauge in one 24 hour period in 1886, and the line in Texas was standard gauged on January 12, 1887. Hard times, wrecks, and washouts plagued the St. Louis, Arkansas & Texas Ry. and following a receivership, it was reorganized in 1891 as the St. Louis Southwestern Railway. Through acquisition of stock, the road is now controlled by the Southern Pacific.

(Courtesy of St. Louis Southwestern Railway)

KANSAS & GULF SHORT LINE RAILROAD was organized in 1880 and authorized to build a railway from Tyler, Texas, south to Sabine Pass on the Gulf of Mexico. In January, 1881, the road acquired the properties of the Rusk Transportation Co., a narrow gauge wooden tram road operated by horse power between Rusk and Jacksonville, Texas. The Kansas & Gulf Short Line extended this line north to Tyler in 1882, and replaced the wooden rails with metal ones. The line from Rusk south to Lufkin, Texas, was completed in July, 1885. It was deeded to the St. Louis, Arkansas & Texas Railway in 1887, but this deed was voided by a legal order and the line was deeded to the Tyler Southeastern Railway in 1891. The 90-odd miles of track was widened to standard gauge in 1895 and the road was acquired as the Lufkin Branch of the St. Louis Southwestern Railway Co. of Texas in 1899. Engine No. 4 of the Kansas & Gulf Short Line Railroad is shown here with an ante-bellum porticoed house in the tree-shaded background. The 2-6-0 was built by Brooks in 1880, was a narrow gauge woodburner, and was sold in 1886.

(Courtesy of St. Louis Southwestern Railway)

TEXAS & PACIFIC RAILWAY was chartered in March, 1871, as the successor to the Texas Pacific Railroad. The road acquired the properties of several Texas short lines, including the Southern Transcontinental Railway and the Southern Pacific Railroad. The Southern Transcontinental was a reorganization of the old Memphis, El Paso & Pacific, a road financed by the noted explorer, John Charles Fremont. The Civil War brought hard times to this road and in 1870 a shipment of 10 locomotives, built in the Andre Koechlin Works, Mulhausen, Alsace, France, were diverted when word reached Europe that the road was in financial straits. The Southern Pacific Railroad acquired by the Texas & Pacific was no kin of the present S P.; it was an outgrowth of the charter issued to the Texas Western in 1852, and constructed some trackage from Caddo Lake, near Shreveport, Louisiana, west toward Marshall, Texas. The Texas & Pacific was led by President Thomas Scott in its early days, with Maj.-Gen. Grenville M. Dodge of Union Pacific fame as Chief Engineer. It later became a Gould property and extended across Texas, using joint track with the Galveston, Harrisburg & San Antonio from Sierra Blanca to El Paso, 92 miles. Fred Jukes, venerable rail photographer, used a box camera to capture Texas & Pacific Engine 116 at Shreveport, Louisiana, in 1898, the year Supt. of Motive Power Jno. Addis completed her in the Marshall, Texas, shops. Note the lagged smokebox, sand dome eagle, and script lettering, plus the early Pyle electric light.

(Courtesy of Fred Jukes)

TEXAS & PACIFIC'S ENGINE 34 is admired by small fry as she heads a string of varnish at Lawrence Siding, Texas, in 1888. The 4-4-0, bearing Pittsburgh's Shop No. 357, was built in 1876.

PITTSBURGH LOCOMOTIVE WORKS built No. 78 for the Texas & Pacific in August, 1880; the 4-6-0 carried Shop No. 417. Note the extended smokebox and the patent stack, a pipe from the latter applied to carry cinders down the left side of the engine and deposit them on the roadbed. A set of mudguards cover the main and forward drivers, and a second set covers the rear drivers located under the wooden cab. (Both photos, Collection of Dr. S. R. Wood)

HOT SPRINGS RAILROAD, sometimes known as the Hot Springs Branch, was a narrow gauge line extending for 25 miles from Malvern to Hot Springs, Arkansas. It was operated as a branch of the St. Louis, Iron Mountain, and Southern Railway, and was opened for service in November of 1875. The road left the Iron Mountain at Malvern, 388 miles south from St. Louis, and served the famous spa resort at Hot Springs, a favored watering spot in days long gone by. Engine No. 2, shown here at the ornate brick depot located in Hot Springs, was named the DIAMOND JO and was built by the Porter works in September, 1875, bearing Shop No. 227. This photo of the neat little slim-gauge woodburner was taken in 1877; in 1889 she was sold to the Missouri Southern and renamed MURILL SPRINGS.   (Collection of Dr. S. R. Wood)

ST. LOUIS, HANNIBAL & KEOKUK RAILROAD was chartered around 1872 and by 1878 was operating 39 miles of standard gauge track from Hannibal to Bowling Green, Missouri. By 1882 the line was in operation from Hannibal to Gilmore, Missouri; at Gilmore it connected with the old North Missouri Railroad, which had become the St. Louis, Kansas City & Northern Ry. and then the Wabash, St. Louis & Pacific. In 1892 a branch line 18 miles long was opened from Ralls Junction to Perry, Missouri, giving the line a total of 103 miles of track. Around the turn of the century the line, restyled the St. Louis & Hannibal Railway, had 9 locomotives and 127 cars on its roster. Engine No. 8, shown here, was built for the St. Louis, Hannibal & Keokuk in 1885 by Schenectady Locomotive Works. The diamond stacked 4-4-0 bore builder's number 1932.   (Collection of Dr. S. R. Wood)

MISSOURI SOUTHERN RAILROAD, operating a 3 foot gauge pike, was the successor to the Mill Spring, Current River & Barnesville Railroad in 1887. The road eventually was extended from Leeper to Ellington, with a branch to the Lone Star Mill. Engine No. 1, the ELLINGTON, was a trim little woodburning Mogul, shown here at the head end of a passenger train consisting of a coach and a combine. The absence of uniforms on the train crew hints at the easy-going informality of short line operations on this slim-gauge trackage.

MISSISSIPPI RIVER & BONNE TERRE RAILWAY was incorporated May 11, 1888, under the laws of the State of Missouri. On March 10, 1890, the 46 miles of standard gauge road was opened for service between Riverside and Doe Run, Missouri. In 1893 the Richmond Locomotive Works turned out Engine 21 for the line, a neat 4-4-0 bearing Richmond Shop No. 2390. The Mississippi River & Bonne Terre offered both freight and passenger service, and conected with the St. Louis, Iron Mountain & Southern at Riverside and at Doe Run Junction. In 1905 the line had a stud of 19 locomotives, and the rolling stock included 760 dump cars for handling mining products. The road served the villages of Genevieve, Bonne Terre, Flat River, and Valles Mines; near Festus, the Crystal Railroad crossed the Bonne Terre line on its way from Silica to Crystal City, Missouri.

(Collection of Dr. S. R. Wood)

ST. LOUIS COAL RAILROAD'S Engine 10 posed for this photo at Belleville, Illinois. The pretty ten-wheeler was built by the Rome Works in 1884 and bore Shop No. 98. (Collection of Dr. S. R. Wood)

FINE EXAMPLE of the locomotive build-
ers art was No. 3 of the Cherokee Iron &
R.R. Co., an 0-4-2 tank type named the
BELLE WEST. She was built by Bald-
win in 1880, Shop No. 4947.
(Collection of Dr. S. R. Wood)

BOOMER RAILROAD OFFICIALS were not frequently encountered in the American West; although a few of the species
existed, their numbers were limited and the yarns of the region deal mostly with the exploits of boomer train, engine, and
yard men, along with telegraphers and machinists. One forgotten example of the boomer brass hat was W. H. Pettibone.
Born March 30, 1840, Mr. Pettibone served as a passenger conductor on the Old Atlantic & Great Western before starting
his long career as an official. He was General Superintendent of the Toledo, Cincinnati & St. Louis Railway and served in
the same capacity on the Burlington, Cedar Rapids & Minnesota Railroad. He held the position of Asst. Gen. Mgr. on the
Atlantic & Danville Railway and served as Superintendent of the Adirondack & St. Lawrence Railway and the Mohawk &
Malone Railway, and was General Supt. of the Toledo, St. Louis & Kansas City Railroad. Mr. Pettibone is also believed
to have been a Division Superintendent or perhaps General Superintendent on the Atchison, Topeka & Santa Fe in the
early 1870's, and served as General Manager for a trunk line in Mexico. He retired and settled in Redlands, California,
where T. C. Peck appointed him passenger and ticket agent for the Salt Lake Route around 1916. Mr. Pettibone retired
from this post about 3 years before he passed away on December 6, 1936, being then nearly 97 years old; his remains were
taken to his old home in Arcade, New York, for burial. This photo shows Mr. Pettibone, at far right, at Dupont, Ohio, in
1887, when he was Gen. Supt. of the T. St.L. & K.C.; business car 99 is hauled by Eng. 1, a Porter 2-4-0 built in 1874. The
little narrow gauge locomotive, bearing Porter's Shop No. 203, was originally the Toledo & Maumee Narrow Gauge Railroad's No. 2, later becoming Toledo, Delphos & Burlington's No. 2 before being acquired by the Toledo, St. Louis & Kansas City Railroad as their No. 1. This photograph was taken on March 30, 1887, the 47th anniversary of Mr. Pettibone's
birthday; although he was rather feeble physically in his last years, his mind was keen and alert. What a vast fund of
pioneer rail lore was lost when this grand old gentleman passed to his reward.   (Collection of Dr. S. R. Wood)

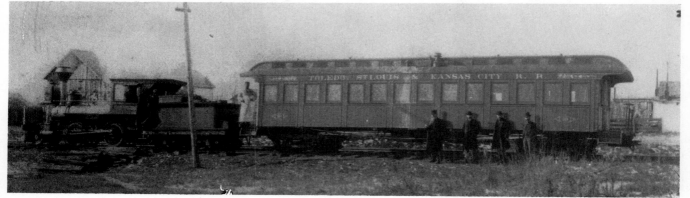

Memories Of The Katy

Engine 71 poses on the transfer table at the Katy's old stone back-shops at Parsons about 1894. She was a 4-4-0 by Rogers, built in 1873, Shop No. 2449.

Engine 72, a 4-4-0 built by Baldwin, Shop No. 4014, was new in 1876. She is shown here with the Parsons shop force; a touch of the Wild West is added by the call boy, mounted on the horse at left. (All photos, Collection of Dr. S. R. Wood)

MISSOURI, KANSAS & TEXAS RAILWAY started life as the Union Pacific Railway Company, Southern Branch, chartered in 1865. This original group planned to build from near the junction of the Smoky Hill and Republican forks of the Kansas River, near Fort Riley, to the point at or near where the Neosho River was crossed by the southern border of Knasas, eventually to be extended south to New Orleans. The name was changed to the Missouri, Kansas & Texas Railway Co. in 1870, actual construction having begun under the original name at Junction City, Kansas, on October 15, 1867. Eastern investors, including Judge Levi Parsons, L. P. Morton, August Belmont, and others, joined Col. Robert Stevens in pushing the Katy in it's race against James F. Joy's Border Tier road in the rush to Indian lands. The Katy passed through Council Grove and Emporia, joining a branch built by the subsidiary Tebo & Neosho and the Labette & Sedalia companies at a company-owned townsite that was named Parsons, Kansas. The Katy built south into Oklahoma and Texas, passed in and out of Jay Gould's control, and continues to serve the southwest well   Engine 18 of the MK&T is shown here at the Parsons depot about 1880 with a passenger train. The 4-4-0 was built by Schenectady, Shop No. 664, in 1870 and was scrapped in 1898. Much of the early Katy track was laid by an Irish contractor, John Scullin, a two-fisted, fighting railroad construction man who later founded the Scullin Steel Company of St. Louis.   (Courtesy of Dr. S. R. Wood)

KANSAS CITY & PACIFIC RAILWAY was chartered on July 24, 1886, to construct a line north from Parsons, Kansas. One of the prime movers in the formation of this company was Colonel Robert S. Stevens, who had been the first General Manager of the Missouri, Kansas & Texas. By 1887, Stevens' Kansas City & Pacific had constructed 95 miles of track due north of Parsons to Paola, Kansas, where the new road connected with the Kansas City, Fort Scott & Gulf; by an agreement with the latter, trains of the K.C. & P. were given trackage rights to Coffeyville and Kansas City. Later leased to the Katy after the Gould regime ended, the road was consolidated into the M.K. & T. Lines in July, 1899. Katy's No. 124, a 4-4-0 shown here at Hartford, Kansas, in 1905, was originally Kansas City & Pacific's No. 55, built by the Dickson Works in 1889, Shop No. 695. She first became M.K. & T. No. 305, was renumbered 124 in December, 1895, and in 1921 was re-numbered 327; she was dismantled at Parsons in December, 1921.   Courtesy of Dr. S. R. Wood)

ALL ABOARD FOR HANNIBAL! Engine No. 75 of the Missouri, Kansas & Texas stands at the Missouri Pacific depot in Sedalia, Missouri, ready to depart for Hannibal with a string of varnish. The crew in this photo taken around 1890 included Conductor H. J. Smith, Engineer De Las McComas, and Fireman Charles Parks. Engine 75 was built by Baldwin in 1876, bearing Shop No. 4019. (Collection of Dr. S. R. Wood)

MISSOURI, KANSAS & TEXAS RAILWAY'S Engine No. 14 was a diamond stack 4-4-0 built by Pittsburgh in 1870, bearing builders' number 83. She is shown here on the old main line near the Parsons & Pacific Railway roundhouse, just south of the Kansas City, Fort Scott & Memphis Railway crossing, on March 2, 1894. No. 14 was just out of the shops, having been repaired following a collision with Engine 64. (Collection of Dr. S. R. Wood)

"WELCOME TO TEXAS" proclaims the sign on the running board of MK&T Engine 202. The photo of this decorated Mogul was taken at Denison, Texas, in 1891 when the engine was dolled up for a state tour of the delegates to the National Convention of the Order of Railway Conductors; note the big ORC emblem on the cab, beneath the fancy fringed arm-rest. Engineer J. T. Adler stands with his long oiler at the left of the main driver. Engine 202 was brand new the year this picture was taken, having been built for the Katy by Baldwin, Shop No. 11733. She was later renumbered 134 and was dismantled at Parsons, Kansas, in December of 1913. (Collection of Dr. S. R. Wood)

KNIGHT TEMPLAR EXCURSION provided the reason for the fancy job of decorating Engine 296 of the Katy; note the open Bible on the pilot beam between the two pillars and directly below the crown and cross fixed on the smokebox. This photo of the high-stepping Atlantic type was taken at the shops in Parsons, Kansas, in August, 1895. No. 296 was only about a month old at the time, having been constructed by Baldwin in July, 1895, under Shop No. 14346. The small splasher boxes located on the running board over her drivers is slightly reminiscent of English motive power of the period. (Collection of Dr. S. R. Wood)

NEITHER HELL NOR HIGH WATER daunted the early Western railroader. Indian attacks, floods, blizzards, prairie or forest fires, he met them head-on and asked for no quarter. This rare old action photo was taken on May 29, 1896, and shows a Katy passenger train easing along through the overflow of the flooding Osage River. The picture was taken near Schell City, Missouri, a station on the Missouri, Kanas & Texas named for the New York bankers, Richard and Augustus Schell. This station proved to be the nucleus of a new town, drawing most of the inhabitants and business firms from the old town of Beloit, located a short distance away and by-passed by the railroad. The 4-4-0 with the diamond stack so bravely nosing through the flood is the MK&T No. 30, built by Grant in 1871 and scrapped on December 10, 1900.

(Collection of Dr. S. R. Wood)

DECKED OUT WITH FLAGS AND BANNERS, the Katy's No. 82 heads an excursion train prior to 1894. She was built by Baldwin in 1877, Shop No. 4110, and later renumbered 338, being cut up in 1913.

(Collection of Dr. S. R. Wood)

Engine 41 was an 0-4-0 tank switcher built by Grant in 1873.

Engine 54, a Mason 4-4-0 built in 1873 and photographed in 1875.

Engine 80, a 4-4-0 built by Baldwin in 1877, Shop No. 4157. Photo taken in 1887 when in passenger service. (All photos, collection of Dr. S. R. Wood)

Engine 75, shown here about 1885, was a 4-4-0 built by Baldwin in 1876, Shop No. 4019.

Second 200, a Mogul built by Baldwin in 1892, Shop No. 12678. This 2-6-0 was a Vauclain compound, the first compound on the Katy.

Fourth No. 1, the TEXAS, at Iola, Kansas, in 1904. An ex-Missouri Pacific 4-4-0 built by Baldwin. Originally Katy's 322, she was rebuilt and used as an inspection engine for officials in 1913. Rebuilt to a regular 4-4-0 in 1916. Later sold to the Eastland, Wichita Falls & Gulf Railway. (All photos, collection of Dr. S. R. Wood)

THE BORDER TIER ROAD, projected by James Joy, was officially named the Missouri River, Fort Scott & Gulf Railroad. Organized in 1868 and opened from Kansas City to Baxter Springs in 1870, the line lost its race into Indian Territory to the Katy, due to political pressure. The road was the parent of the Kansas City, Fort Scott & Memphis, later part of the St. Louis & San Francisco. Engine 7 (top) a Manchester built in 1869, bore that number under both MRFS&G and KCFS&M ownership; photo at Thayer, Mo., in 1888. Engine 19 (center) a Manchester product of 1870, also carried the same road number under both ownerships. KCFS&M 111 (bottom) was a 4-6-0 built by Pittsburgh in 1892 and is shown at Mountain Grove, Missouri, in 1893.
(All photos, collection of Dr. S. R. Wood) Engine 75, shown here about 1885, was a 4-4-0 built by Baldwin in 1876, Shop No. 4019.

ST. LOUIS & SAN FRANCISCO RAILWAY was organized on September 7, 1876, as the successor of the old Atlantic & Pacific Railroad of 1866. Included in the property was the South Pacific Railroad, the former Southwest Branch of the Pacific Railroad of Missouri, organized in March, 1868. By 1871 the road was opened from Pacific Junction, Missouri, to Vinita, Indian Territory, a distance of 326.50 miles. The standard gauge line was laid with 56 pound iron and included over 19 miles of steel rail by 1878; over 30 miles of sidings existed along the original line. Following a reorganization in 1896, the Frisco acquired numerous short lines giving it a web of steel in Missouri, Kansas, Indian Territory, Oklahoma, Arkansas, Tennessee, and Alabama, with subsidiaries in Texas. Frisco's Engine 31, a diamond stacked 4-4-0, is shown popping off at the head end of 5 wooden coaches near the portal of Winslow Tunnel, Arkansas.

(Collection of Dr. S. R. Wood)

Frisco Motive Power

Diamond stacked trio of Baldwin engines used on the Saint Louis & San Francisco Railroad, all using crosshead water pumps.

Engine 2, an 0-6-0 switcher, was built in 1881, later renumbered 1642 and 3642
Engine 44 was a 4-6-0 built in 1879 with mudguards over her engine trucks as well as over her drivers.

Engine 68 was a husky 2-8-0 built in 1881. Later numbers borne by this Consolidation included 268,702, and 2702.

(All photos, collection of Dr. S. R. Wood)

Early Days On The St. Louis & San Francisco

Frisco's 50 and 132 at the old Kansas Southwestern's roundhouse at Anthony, Kansas, in 1890. This line ran east for 159 miles to Arkansas City, Kansas, and is now a Santa Fe branch.

Frisco's No. 65 was a Rogers 4-4-0 built in 1880 and named the CAPT. C. W. ROGERS, in honor of an early General Superintendent.

Frisco 158 was built by Baldwin in 1879, a 4-6-0 that was originally St. L. & S. F. No. 48. She later was renumbered 408. Note the hewn ties and the lack of ballast.

(All photos, collection of Dr. S. R. Wood)

AFTER THE CHASE, this 4-4-0 and a group of railroaders posed for a photographer at Frederick, Oklahoma, in 1905. The decorated engine is No. 2234 of the St. Louis-San Francisco, and she had just completed what probably was the longest railroad hunt in history. This engine pulled a train bearing President Theodore Roosevelt on a coyote hunt from Vernon, Texas, to Frederick, Oklahoma, with the noted sportsman banging away at the coyotes infesting the region. The 2234 was originally built by Manchester in 1870; after having borne number 8 on the Kansas City, Fort Scott & Memphis, she became No 234 of the St. Louis & San Francisco before being renumbered 2234. The rather rumpled condition of the bunting decorating the locomotive seems to indicate that her hogger let her out a bit in order to bring some speedy coyote within range of the Presidential gunsight. (Collection of Dr. S. R. Wood)

"THE SLICKER" was the nickname applied to this Frisco accomodation train which made two round trips daily between Mansfield and Fort Smith, Arkansas. The train is shown here at the portal of Jensen Tunnel in 1890, headed by St. Louis & San Francisco's Engine 32, a polished 4-4-0 with a cinder blow-off device visible in front of her right steam chest. Engineer George Daniels is seated at the latch, and Fireman John Yocum stands in the 32's gangway; the uniformed skipper leaning on the pilot beam is Conductor A. Greenwood, with Brakeman T. W. Crittenden standing at his left. The small engine and wooden cars are typical of the thousands of local passenger schedules that ran on short turnaround jobs in the West in a happier day, before the hard-surfaced road and the gas engine drove them into oblivion. (Collection of Dr. S. R. Wood)

FRISCO'S ENGINE 44 turned over at Sarcoxie, Missouri, in 1882, demolishing her wooden cab and breaking her diamond stack loose from the smokebox. Engineer F. S. Potter was at the throttle when the 4-6-0 bit the dust. The tenwheeler, equipped with the conventional crosshead cold water pump, was built by Baldwin in 1879.

THE HARD WAY to turn a locomotive is illustrated in this view taken at Cordell, Oklahoma, in 1902. On a crude turntable composed of two lengths of rail, a few ties, and some small rollers that appear to be sections of pipe, the huskies manning the pinch bars and levers are giving the tender of Engine 2 a ride on their primitive merry-go-'round. The tender has been uncoupled from the locomotive and each had to be turned separately, due to the short length of the improvised turning facilities. The 4-4-0, reportedly acquired from the Union Pacific, is shown bearing the initials of the Blackwell, Enid & South Western Railway, an auxiliary of the St. Louis & San Francisco Railroad. The line, 238 miles long, ran from Blackwell, Oklahoma Territory, to Red River, Texas; other Frisco-controlled roads radiating from Red River were the Blackwell, Enid & Texas Ry., Oklahoma City & Texas R.R., and the Paris & Great Northern R.R. The Frisco also controlled the Ozark & Cherokee Central Ry., Fort Worth & Rio Grande Ry., Arkansas Valley & Western Ry., and the St. Louis, San Francisco & New Orleans Railroad.

(Collection of Dr. S. R. Wood)

FLOODING WASHITA RIVER weakened a bridge south of Cordell, Oklahoma, in 1907, with the tragic results shown here. Frisco's Eng. 312, a Baldwin Mogul built in 1887, plunged through the span and landed in the swirling flood. Fireman Gody, standing in the gangway when the engine fell into the water, had his hand caught between the tender and cab and was drowned. A relief train engine is visible beyond the tender of the wrecked Mogul, her smoke drifting off across the inundated bottomlands.

(Collection of Dr. S. R. Wood)

KANSAS CITY, PITTSBURG & GULF RAILROAD was built to tap the mining regions around Pittsburg and Joplin, Missouri, but under the guiding hand of Arthur Stilwell the road was bolstered by Dutch capital and extended south. Stilwell, born in Rochester, New York, in 1859, became president of the road at the age of 32 and helped the line weather the panic of 1893. A southern terminus on the waters of the Gulf of Mexico was planned and the road considered acquiring the Houston, East & West Texas, but Stilwell was not pleased with Galveston as a port site and the road built to Lake Sabine, where the new terminal was located and named Port Arthur. The railroad then opened the Port Arthur Channel to the Gulf, a waterway later taken over by the Government. Engine 1 of the Kansas City, Pittsburg & Gulf was a husky Baldwin 4-4-0, Shop No. 14443, built in September, 1895. She later became No. 107 of the successor Kansas City Southern and was scrapped at Shreveport, Louisiana, in 1915. This photo shows that she came from the Baldwin Works equipped with an air bell ringer, cap stack, and link and pin coupler; she had 18 x 24 inch cylinders and 63 inch drivers. (Collection of Dr. S. R. Wood)

KANSAS CITY, FORT SMITH & SOUTHERN RAILWAY was possibly the only railroad in the United States to be constructed by an Indian. Mathias Splitlog owned a valuable tract of land around the mouth of the Kaw River in Wyandotte County, Kansas, which he sold for a sizeable chunk of cash. The Kansas City stockyards and packing plants are located on this property. With the profits from this real estate transaction, Splitlog organized the Kansas City, Fort Smith & Southern in 1887, with the ambitious idea of extending it through Indian Territory to the Gulf of Mexico. The road was constructed from Joplin, Missouri, south to Goodman, a distance of about 30 miles. At Goodman, the line ran west for about 4 miles to Splitlog City, a town the chief was developing. Crooked promoters sold Splitlog a "salted" gold mine and when the swindle was exposed, he became disgusted and sold the railway to eastern interests. The short section from Goodman to Splitlog City was torn up and the line extended southward to Sulphur Springs, Arkansas, by the new owners. In October, 1893, the line was purchased by the Kansas City, Pittsburg & Gulf and became a part of their main line. This photo shows Engine 2 of the "Splitlog Road," a trim 4-4-0 built by Brooks, Shop No. 1532, in April, 1889; she had 17 x 24 inch cylinders and 61 inch drivers. In 1894 the engine became KCP&G's No. 10, later becoming Kansas City Southern No. 132, and going to the scrapper in 1910. (Courtesy of Kansas City Southern Lines)

LINK IN THE GULF ROUTE projected by Arthur Stilwell was the Texarkana & Fort Smith Railroad; the emblem on the tank of the 4-4-0 shown here bears the legend, "Port Arthur Route," although Engine 5 carries the Texarkana & Fort Smith initials on her cab panel. In 1885 a Texarkana lumberman, W. L. Whitaker, organized the Texarkana & Northern Railroad to tap additional timber holdings. The line extended north of Texarkana and bridged the Red River and in 1889 was renamed the Texarkana & Fort Smith. Whitaker planned to extend the road north to Fort Smith, Arkansas, but his Eastern backing failed and he suggested that the line might fit into Stilwell's plans for a route from Kansas City to the Gulf of Mexico. The Stilwell road, then operating as the Kansas City, Nevada & Fort Smith Railroad, acquired Whitaker's line and the merged companies became the Kansas City, Pittsburg & Gulf Railroad. This photo shows Texarkana & Fort Smith's Engine No. 5 with a work train on the trestle approach to the Arkansas River bridge at Redland, Oklahoma, probably before the turn of the century.   (Courtesy of Kansas City Southern Lines)

DEPOT AT RICH MOUNTAIN, ARKANSAS, forms the setting for this view of KCP&G Engine 140 and a passenger train in 1900. The 4-4-0 was originally KCP&G No. 11. Engineer Walter Hoag is at the throttle in this photo.

(Collection of Dr. S. R. Wood)

THE PANIC OF 1893 caused American investors to tighten their purse strings, resulting in the loss of fresh capital for railroad construction. Acting on one of his famed "hunches," Arthur Stilwell set sail for Holland, where he sold the entire bond issue of $3,000,000 necessary to connect up his Kansas City, Pittsburg & Gulf and complete the line to the Port Arthur terminus. As a result of this influx of Dutch capital, many Holland Dutch names dotted the "Port Arthur Route"; these included Amsterdam, Missouri, and Hornbeck, Zwolle, DeRidder, and DeQuincy, Louisiana. In Arkansas, the town of DeQueen bore the Anglicized version of DeGeoijen, in honor of John DeGeoijen, the Dutch coffee merchant who helped Stilwell peddle the stock. Other Arkansas towns showing the Dutch influence were Vandervoort and Mena, the latter being credited as the name of both Mrs. DeGeoijen and the nickname of Queen Wilhelmina of The Netherlands. This 1896 view shows a "P&G" passenger train at Mena, Arkansas, headed by Engine 11 of the Kansas City, Pittsburg & Gulf. The big 4-4-0 was built by Schenectady, Shop No. 4167, in 1893 and renumbered 140, later becoming Kansas City Southern's 140. She had 18 x 24 inch cylinders, 63 inch drivers, and was scrapped at Pittsburg in July, 1939. Note the sketchy grade and the lack of ballast in the hastily-constructed track; poor quality of original construction was to cause trouble for the road for many years.

(Collection of Dr. S. R. Wood)

IT WAS CHRISTMAS DAY and Engineer Walter Hoag was pounding along the rough, unballasted main stem of the Kansas City, Pittsburg & Gulf with old No. 12 and the morning passenger train, scorching the light iron laid without benefit of tie plates. Topping Neosho Hill at 8:31 A.M. on that 25th of December, 1894, the wheels hit the ties and No. 12 ploughed up the Missouri earth as she rolled onto her right side and nosed along the roadbed. The wooden coaches remained upright and Walter Hoag survived the spill to handle the latch on many more P&G varnish runs. Engine 12 was a 4-4-0 built by Schenectady in 1893, bearing Shop No. 4168. The Kansas City, Pittsburg & Gulf later renumbered her 141, a number she retained under Kansas City Southern ownership. She was dismantled at Pittsburg, Kansas, on April 1, 1914. Note the star painted on her smokebox and the slightly awed expressions on the faces of the numerous small fry of the "Show Me" State, gathered to witness the local catastrophe.   (Collection of Dr. S. R. Wood)

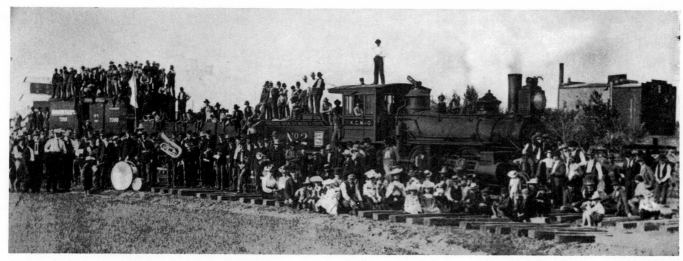

KANSAS CITY, MEXICO & ORIENT RAILROAD was incorporated in May, 1900, by Arthur Stilwell and others, and proposed to build a standard gauge road from Kansas City, Missouri, to Topolobampo, Mexico, on the Gulf of California. Stilwell, just ousted from the Kansas City, Pittsburg & Gulf, was not the first to dream of such a rail link; Albert K. Owen had envisioned a railway from some Atlantic seaboard terminal to Topolobampo Bay as early as 1872. He succeeded in organizing the Texas, Topolobampo & Pacific R.R. after having interested President U. S. Grant in the route, and some grading was done around Topolobampo in 1885, but the dream failed and the project died. Stilwell enlisted the aid of Mexico's President Porfirio Diaz and Enrique C. Creel, head of the Chihuahua & Pacific Railway, and was granted a concession to operate in Mexico. Construction was started on five segments in 1902 in the United States and Mexico, the first section opened being the 74 miles from Milton, Kansas, south to Carmen, Oklahoma. A great deal of public support was given Stilwell's project and when the first train rolled into Anthony, Kansas, in 1903, a big crowd and a band turned out to celebrate. Engine 2, surrounded by the well-wishers, was a 2-6-0 Dickson of uncertain ancestry. She is lettered: "Ferrocarril Kansas City, Mexico y Oriente" and the herald on her tank reads: "Port Stilwell Route." Just as he had located Port Arthur, Texas, for his KCP&G line, Stilwell had located the Mexican terminus of the Orient on a landlocked harbor, hence the name Port Stilwell.   (Collection of Dr. S. R. Wood)

KANSAS CITY, PITTSBURG & GULF purchased Eng. 364 from the Baldwin factory in 1898. The 4-6-0 became Kansas City Southern's 364 and was dismantled at Pittsburg, Kansas, in 1925.   (Collection of Dr. S. R. Wood)

ARTHUR STILWELL'S DREAM of a railroad from Kansas City to the West Coast of Mexico nearly became a reality in the early 1900's. Construction was pushed on the various disconnected sections of the Orient route, although the track was largely unballasted. Trackage rights over the Kansas & Colorado Pacific carried the Orient trains from Milton north to Wichita, Kansas, and the Panhandle & Gulf Railway in Texas took over the old Colorado Valley Railroad to build from Sweetwater to San Angelo. Connection between the Texas lines and the Orient's main stem from Kansas across Oklahoma was made in late 1908, when the Red River bridge was completed. The line reached San Angelo, Texas, in June of 1909; on the Pacific end, the road had been opened from Topolobampo to Fuerte, 62 miles, in 1904 and the Minaca-Sanchez section was completed shortly thereafter, while the Chihuahua-Falomir line was finished by 1908. One big obstacle was the Sierra Madres, where grades were so steep that a 40 mile cog railway section was first proposed; later surveys located an easier rounte through the Mexican mountains, but that section was never completed. The revolt that deposed President Diaz from power in Mexico was led by Pancho Villa, a former contractor on the Oriente line, and the revolutionaries tied up the Mexican operations. Unable to meet the interest on bonds due, the Orient went into receivership in 1912 and Stilwell's vision crumbled to dust. Engine 20, shown here, was an 0-6-0 bought new from Alco-Pittsburgh in 1909, when the Orient was booming; photo was taken at San Angelo in 1914.
(Collection of Dr. S. R. Wood)

ST. LOUIS, IRON MOUNTAIN & SOUTHERN'S No. 587 was a 4-6-0 built by Rogers, Shop No. 5315, in 1898. She later became Missouri Pacific's No. 2514.
(Collection of Dr. S. R. Wood)

ORIENT VARNISH is headed by Engine 505, an American Standard built by Alco (Cooke Works) in 1907. This engine, along with a number of others used on the KCM&O, was equipped with Allfree-Hubbell valves; she had 18 x 26 inch cylinders and 69 inch drivers. After receivership and reorganization, the Orient had financial ups and downs, including a spurt of business in the 1920's when oil wells began spouting black gold at the Big Lake, McCamey, Yates, and the Church-Fields-McElroy oil fields. Some new construction was started on the lines in Mexico, assisted by the Mexican government as reparation for the damages wrought by Villa's revolutionaries. In 1928 the Atchison, Topeka & Santa Fe gained control of the Orient lines in the United States, extending the road to the Rio Grande at Presidio and completing the San Angelo-Sonora branch in 1930. The three divisions of the old Stillwell road in Mexico were sold in 1928 to B. F. Johnston, Mexico's sugar magnate, and the lines were reorganized as the Ferrocarril Kansas City, Mexico y Oriente, S.A., and operations were administered by the Mexico Northwestern Railway, a major connecting road. In 1940 the lines in Mexico were acquired by the government of President Cardenas and plans for the completion of the original Orient route are still being tossed around by various political factions. The old Orient was quite a stomping-ground for boomer railroaders who, for various reasons, found work there that could not be obtained in the States, but most of these American railroaders were forced to flee when Pancho Villa overthrew the Diaz regime.

(Collection of Dr. S. R. Wood)

ATLANTIC & PACIFIC RAILROAD steel crawls west through the pinelands of New Mexico in the early 1880's. This old photograph depicts the hewn ties strung out on the raw grade, while the gang of men and the construction train push the end of track toward the setting sun. The husky laborers carried the rail into position on the ties and pairs of spike drivers swung their mauls in rhythmical cadence, anchoring the rail to the cross ties. Angle bars bolted in place, the crew moved steadily forward, followed by the funnel-stacked locomotive and the flat cars loaded with material. Coupled behind the tender of the engine is an auxiliary water car to furnish additional water for the boiler of the work train locomotive.

(Courtesy of Santa Fe Railway)

SCENIC GRANDEUR OF MOUNTAIN RAILROADING is captured in this Colorado view from the camera of the noted Wm. H. Jackson. Taken in Chalk Creek Canyon near St. Elmo around 1883, this photograph shows a mixed train on the Denver, South Park & Pacific, headed by Engine No. 3. This engine, a 2-6-6T type, was the first of the Mason Bogies acquired by the South Park, and bore the name, ORO CITY. Built for the road in May, 1878, she had 13 x 16 inch cylinders, 37 inch drivers, and weighed 43,850 pounds on her driving wheels. She carried Mason Shop No. 591, became Eng. No. 40 of the Denver, Leadville & Gunnison operations, and was scrapped in 1890. The South Park followed up Chalk Creek Canyon west of Nathrop on it's climb to Alpine Tunnel, en route to Gunnison and the branch lines leading to Kubler and Baldwin.
(W. H. Jackson photo, courtesy of Denver Public Library Western Collection)

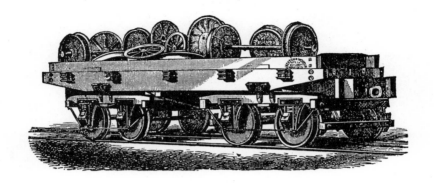

Rails
Through the Rockies.

Railroading in the region surrounding the Rocky Mountains has probably captured the fancy of more rail enthusiasts than any other section of the United States. There are several likely reasons for the strong appeal this area holds. Here was the heart of America's narrow gauge kingdom, where men of iron determination battled Nature and all her obstacles with diminutive engines and trains calculated to endear them to generations of railroad devotees.

FIRST LOCOMOTIVE for General William J. Palmer's narrow gauge Denver & Rio Grande Railroad was the little 2-4-0 type named the MONTEZUMA, built by Baldwin in 1871. Shown here at the Baldwin factory before delivery to the infant Colorado road, the little No. 1 sported 9 x 16 inch cylinders, 40 inch drivers, and tipped the scales to a total weight of 25,000 pounds; her builder's plates carried Baldwin Shop No. 2459. Her sister 2-4-0's, built for the Rio Grande by Baldwin in 1871, were No.'s 4, the CORTEZ; 6, the UTE; and 7, the DEL NORTE. The Colorado Eastern Railway, a 17-mile pike built from Denver to Scranton in 1886, acquired D. & R. G. No. 6, the UTE, and assigned her the same road number on their roster.

Only a scattered few researchers may be familiar with the Penobscot & Kennebec or the Selma, Rome & Dalton, but the names of the roads that penetrated the Rockies are known the country over . . . Denver & Rio Grande . . . Colorado Midland . . . Florence & Cripple Creek . . . Denver, South Park & Pacific.

Arm-chair railroaders who may have never ventured west of the Hudson or north of Messrs. Mason and Dixon's celebrated line are on speaking terms with the roads of the Rockies, and can expound on the Black Canyon of the Gunnison, the glories of Marshall Pass, Soldier Summit, or the Georgetown Loop. It is not the purpose of this text to recount the corporate histories of the many companies that threaded their rails through the awesome canyons or over the towering peaks. Rather, a few highlights of rail operations will be given in an attempt to recall the early days of puny engines, wooden cars, and the men who laboured, sweated, and sometimes died in their daily struggles to keep the trains rolling.

Railroading in the Colorado Rockies was a game for young men in the early days, and it was not uncommon to see engineers at the throttle who had recently passed their 'teens. Filled with the exuberance and daring of youth, they often charged ahead where older and wiser runners would have hesitated. Such a pair were two engineers on the Denver, South Park & Pacific. A big blizzard in the 1880's caught these

two runners at Gunnison and the South Park line over Alpine Pass was blocked solidly. The Denver & Rio Grande line over Marshall Pass to the east was also blocked and the Rio Grande crews were making futile attempts to open it, since snow conditions there were usually not as severe as those on the Alpine line of the South Park. The South Park men lived in Como, and both were anxious to return home, so they paid a visit to the Rio Grande offices in Gunnison. Here they were granted permission to try to open up the Rio Grande's road over Marshall Pass. The operator at Sargent's, at the foot of the steep climb up Marshall, O.S.'ed them by forty-five finutes after their two South Park kettles had whistled off in Gunnison. About three hours later, the brass pounder at the summit of Marshall Pass rattled his key and notified the dispatcher that the pair of locomotives was standing at his order board. Some two hours later, the South Park boys dropped into Salida, having successfully broken the Rio Grande's blockade. From Salida the two South Park engines were sent up the Rio Grande's line along the Arkansas River to Buena Vista, where they crossed over to the rails of their home road and returned to their terminal.

Other South Park runners were not so fortunate in their combat with the elements. Engineer William Westall hit a gravel slide washed down onto the rails in Platte Canon near Dome Rock and was trapped beneath his overturned

DENVER & RIO GRANDE RAILROAD acquired five Mogul type locomotives built by Baldwin in 1871 for freight service on the new narrow gauge line. These engines were D. & R. G. No. 2, named TABI-WACHI, No. 3, the SHOU-WA-NO, (shown here), No. 5, the OURAY, No. 8, the ARKANSAS, and No. 9, the HUERFANO; three of these engines were later rebuilt to 0-6-0 types. Trailed by 4-wheeled tenders, the Moguls had ornate wooden cabs, diamond stacks, and fancy paint jobs. Water was supplied to their boilers by a crosshead pump on the left side and an injector on the right, which can be noted in this photo of the SHOU-WA-NO. Their specifications included 11 x 16 inch cylinders, 36 inch drivers, and a total weight of 36,000 pounds, 29,000 pounds of which was carried on the mudguard-covered driving wheels.

locomotive. The fireman, Joe Nichols, was thrown clear when the engine rolled over. Billy Westall died in Nichols' arms some twelve hours later still pinned down by the ponderous machine, and his last words were: "Tell my wife I died thinking of her." This accident took place on August 28, 1898, when Westall was pulling a heavily-loaded excursion train. The slide was noticed in ample time to permit him to jump, but Engineer Westall was made of the stuff that stands and stuck to his post in the cab, doing all in his power to avert a bad smash. He succeeded in slowing the train enough before it hit that no passenger was killed, but made the supreme sacrifice while doing his duty.

The Grim Reaper did not always call when the crews were engaged in such heroic actions, however. In 1883 the Rio Grade line through the Black Canon of the Gunnison was plagued by a series of slides caused by a January thaw. A work train was sent out from Gunnison ahead of the westbound morning passenger with a crew of men to dig out the slides. Within the gorge, the work train found a slide and while the section hands were digging it out, the varnished cars came up behind them and stopped on a flag. While standing there, an avalanche of snow hurtled down the steep mountainside and struck the passenger engine, turning it over. Engineer Charles Bratt was suffocated under the tons of white death that buried his engine, and his fireman narrowly escaped a similar fate.

Creeping Death in the mountains would also claim the lives of several railroaders. A cave-in blocked the South Park's Alpine Tunnel in 1888 and seepage formed a small lake inside the tunnel, which was built with a grade leading in both directions from a central apex. Engineer Nathan Martinez and Fireman Michael Byrnes were sent up from Gunnison, on the west side of the pass, to enter the tunnel and siphon this water out to facilitate removing the rock fall. Their engine was the BRECKENRIDGE, one of the Mason Bogies. Ascending the grade from the western portal, they passed the red lamp that marked the summit of the grade, then eased down to the pool backed up behind the cave-in on the eastern slope. While the siphon was being rigged, deadly coal gas from the locomotive filled the dark bore and tragedy was in the making. The unseen fumes claimed the lives of Engineer "Dad" Martinez, Conductor Mike Flavin, Fireman Byrnes, and a laborer named Oscar Cammann. Brakeman Elmer England, a member of the crew, managed to flee the tunnel and escape a similar fate. This accident occurred on June 8, 1895, the tunnel having been blocked for 7 years since the 1888 cave in; in the interim, South Park traffic from the Gunnison end of the road had been routed over the Rio Grande's Marshall Pass line.

The steep grades and poor braking equipment caused many fatal runaways on the pikes traversing the rugged Colorado ranges. In addition to hand brakes, the vacuum brake, Le Chatelier water brake, straight air, and finally, the Westinghouse automatic air brake were all used by the early lines in an effort to give

RIO GRANDE'S ENGINE 87 was one of twelve 4-4-0 type narrow gauge locomotives acquired in 1880, all constructed by the Baldwin Locomotive Works. This engine was named RITO ALTO and carried Baldwin Shop No. 5053; she and a sister engine, No. 92, the MOGOLLON, reportedly were later sold to the Sanford & St. Petersburg Railroad, along with No. 95, the EMBUDA. Note old Towser, the lop-eared hound, standing on the running board. Canine mascots were frequently found amongst railroad surroundings in the early days of the West.

train and engine crews some safe means of controlling their speed down the steep gradients and around the hairpin curves.

In spite of the best efforts of the crews, trains ran away with alarming frequency, often with fatal results. A Rio Grande coal drag got out of control on the east slope of Marshall Pass and ran wild down the mountain, piling up near the siding at Gray's. Fireman Al Boswell and Brakeman Charley Shaw were killed in the crash, Engineer Paddy Ryan died on the way to a hospital, and Brakemen Louis Reed and Johnny Dow were both seriously injured.

Violence in the rough mining camps was commonplace, as witness the following communication, published in the Locomotive Fireman's Magazine in 1887, dated at Como, Colorado, on May 10th:

"Died, at Leadville, May 3rd, 1887, James Clendenning, from a pistol shot fired by one Cagney. James Clendenning became a member of High Line Lodge, 256, on March 5, 1885, and being a charter member, his memory will be cherished by his brother firemen . . . Never, since the great scenic High Line Railroad was constructed over the snowy peaks of the Rocky Mountains, did a braver or truer fireman watch the steam gauge than James P. Clendenning." The Brotherhood of Locomotive Firemen's Committee, composed of Geo. W. McAleer, Walter Mather, and D. Tompkins, further added resolutions expressing sympathy to the survivors of the deceased and thanked the officials of the Denver, South Park & Pacific for furnishing transportation to the relatives and Lodge members to the funeral rites of the murdered fireman. Thanks were also tendered to the members of Cloud City Lodge No. 196, Leadville, and

Rocky Mountain Lodge No. 77, Denver for their kindness in laying away the departed brother. The acts of the railroaders and the officials in connection with the Clendenning death are proof that a closer bond of fellowship seemed to exist between labor and management in those bygone days. Old employees who worked on the roads in the Rockies have commented on the mutual feeling of friendship that existed there, each road and its employees resembling a big family; the Division Superintendent was likely to be found at a slide, wielding a shovel at the elbow of the lowliest gandy dancer; brass hat and section hand, train or engine crews, all had one major aim and that was to keep the trains moving safely over the flimsy track.

And move they did, some Rio Grande engineers hanging up speed records that today's streamliners are hard put to match. The Santa Fe, competing with the Rio Grande for the business between Denver and Pueblo, gave the Rio Grande boys some marks to shoot at in the matter of fast running time. The rivalry between the crews of the Rio Grande and the Colorado Midland also set the stage for some high-wheeling. When the Colorado Midland built west from Glenwood Springs to New Castle, their rails paralleled the established Denver & Rio Grande trackage. From New Castle, the Midland had a joint track agreement with the Rio Grande between that point and Grand Junction. Trains of both roads frequently left Glenwood Springs about the same time, and the first to arrive at New Castle was given the right to enter the single track for the run to Grand Junction. This arrangement caused many an impromptu race as the trains of the two roads roared down toward New Castle, the crews of each eager to get ahead of the other.

While Colorado featured mountain railroading in abundance, other regions had iron rails penetrating the Rockies under conditions equally as hazardous and rivalling Colorado's magnificent scenery. Both the Northern Pacific and the Great Northern, and later, the Milwaukee, pierced the backbone of the Continental Divide in Montana. As on the Colorado roads, snow was the villain in Montana. Miles of snowsheds were erected to shelter the tracks, and periodically the warm Chinooks loosened tons of wet snow, sending the roaring avalanches down to wipe out the railroad and any train unfortunate enough to be caught in their paths.

North of the Line, the Canadian Pacific encountered the same troubles, perhaps on a larger scale due to the terrain and the more northerly location. The slides that engulfed trains on Kicking Horse Pass were just as deadly as those that swept down on the South Park around Woodstock or sent Rio Grande equipment tumbling into the canyons of Cerro Summit or Tennessee Pass.

Falling rocks were a constant source of danger to the men who worked the mountains, with fires in the dry seasons running a close second.

The wooden bridges that spanned most of the many streams were extremely vulnerable to the ravages of fire and more than one mountain crew went to glory when they came boring around a curve only to discover a bed of glowing coals where a bridge or trestle belonged. Flash floods took their toll, churning down the narrow gorges and sweeping rails and bridges away in their savage onslaught.

The narrow gauge lines have all but vanished, and Time has eroded the silent grades where in the brawling, golden yesteryears the polished little Masons, Grants, and Baldwins boomed their exhausts against the rocky ramparts and sent the echoes flying through the gloom of mountain gorges. Trains still roll through the Rockies, but the light iron has given way to heavy steel, and block signals beckon the enginemen ahead, flashing their green indications that the way ahead is safe. If the ghosts of the oldtimers linger around the peaks, they must smile as they witness the drama of modern rail operations, a far cry from the wild old days when they ran on smoke orders, clubbed down hand brakes, and wrote the stories of their goings in a fiery cloud of cinders that spewed into the clear mountain air and fell to earth forgotten.

NARROW GAUGE ELEGANCE is reflected in this view of the Denver & Rio Grande's No. 94, a Baldwin 4-4-0 named the GUNNISON. Built in 1880, Shop No. 5139, the graceful little kettle is respendent with polished dome casings, buck horns mounted on headlight, and striped awnings over the cab window.

THE FIRST CONSOLIDATION TYPE LOCOMOTIVE used on the Denver & Rio Grande was No. 22, the ALAMOSA, built by Baldwin in 1877. This engine was the heaviest class of power to appear on the narrow gauge road since its inception, and she proved so successful that a numerous fleet of 2-8-0 type engines were acquired. One of these, shown here, was No. 33, the SILVER CLIFF. She was built by the Baldwin Works in 1879, bore Shop No. 4504, and had 15 x 18 inch cylinders and 36 inch drivers. Her second and third pairs of drivers were "blind," the tires having no flanges, a feature that reduced rail wear on the sharp curves and contributed to the success of these Consolidations.

DENVER & RIO GRANDE RAILROAD acquired twelve neat 4-4-0 type locomotives built by the Baldwin Works in 1880. No. 88, shown here, bore Shop No. 5198, had 12 x 18 inch cylinders, 45 inch drivers, and carried 130 pounds of working boiler pressure. She was named the PTARMIGAN, while other engines in this group bore such names as RITO ALTO, EAGLE RIVER, WAHSATCH, TEN MILE, MOGOLLON, ROARING FORKS, and GUNNISON.

DEL NORTE, COLORADO, furnished the background for this view of Denver & Rio Grande's No. 95, a trim 4-4-0 named the EMBUDA. Built by Baldwin in 1880, she was a sister to the GUNNISON and carried Shop No. 5140 on her circular builder's plates. Note the single stage air compressor and the main reservoir for the straight air brake, the latter mounted on the sill at the rear of her tank in accordance with D. & R. G. practice. This engine reportedly was sold to the Sanford & St. Petersburg Railroad.

BRITISH IMPORT, the Fairlie type 0-4-4-0 double ender shown here was presented to the Denver & Rio Grande by the Duke of Sutherland and was used on the narrow gauge line over La Veta Pass. Named the MOUNTAINEER and assigned road number 101, the unusual locomotive with two boilers and two separate sets of cylinders and drivers was not very successful, due to excessive slipping. The MOUNTAINEER had 10 x 18 inch cylinders, 39 inch drivers, and weighed 62,000 pounds.

DENVER & RIO GRANDE'S No. 108 was a 3-foot gauge American Standard turned out by Baldwin in 1883, Shop No. 6632. Fred Jukes, that dean of Western railroader-photographers, reports that this engine was a hard coal burner used on the West End of the road, but was not successful in using this type of fuel, due to her inability to steam properly when burning it. Note her tallow cup lubricator mounted on the steam chest, and the "one-lung" or single stage air pump, with the main air reservoir mounted on the rear tender frame behind the tank. The low center of gravity of these slim-gauge engines caused a concentration of valve gear and running gear in such a limited space that there was no room beneath the running boards or under the cab, traditional locations for the air reservoirs, hence the placing of the receptacle at the rear of the tender. Some narrow gauge roads located the reservoirs athwart the boiler, but the result was often an ungainly effect that spoiled the symmetry of the engine's appearance, giving it a cluttered appearance. The 108, nameless on the road's roster, had 12 x 18 inch cylinders, 45 inch drivers, and weighed 44,150 pounds. She later went to the Rio Grande Western Railway.

(Courtesy of Fred Jukes)

THE NARROW GAUGE LINE of the Denver & Rio Grande extending from Denver to Pueblo, Colorado, was the source of trouble and expense, all freight and passenger traffic having to be transferred to the standard gauge connections at these terminals. In 1881 the Rio Grande solved a part of this dilemma by laying a third rail on this route and the line was opened for dual gauge use on January 20th, 1882. To handle the standard gauge passenger operations over the third-rail system, the road acquired three Baldwin 4-6-0 types, all built in 1881. They were numbered 155, 156, and 157, the latter shown here, but were not named. This passenger power had 14 x 20 inch cylinders, 45 inch drivers, and weighed 55,600 pounds.

DENVER & RIO GRANDE'S No. 163 was a trim Baldwin 4-6-0 built in 1882 with Shop No. 5970, one of eight locomotives of this class turned out for the road in that year by Burnham, Parry & Williams These engines weighed 37,650 pounds, had 14 x 20 inch cylinders, and 45 inch drivers. This photograph shows No. 163 sporting a capped stack and antlerdecked headlight; the runner, oiler resting on steam chest, leans nonchalantly on the pilot beam while the fireboy holds his coalburning trade-mark at the gangway.

DENVER & RIO GRANDE'S FAMED "CHILI LINE" ran from Alamosa, Colorado, to the ancient pueblo of Santa Fe, New Mexico, a distance of some 140 miles. Blocked in Raton Pass by the Santa Fe surveyors led by Ray Morley, the Rio Grande built south from Alamosa, reaching Espanola, New Mexico, in 1880. The narrow gauge line chartered the Rio Grande & Santa Fe Railway in 1895 to acquire the old Santa Fe Southern Railroad's 34 miles of road from Espanola south to Santa Fe. Leaving the Alamosa-Durango line at Antonito, the "Chili Line" ran through a region rich in Spanish names, cluding Alcalde, Barranca, Servilleta, and Tres Piedras, following down the valley of the Rio Grande. Of interest along the route were the ancient cliff dwellings, one of which can be faintly noticed at the upper left in this photo, a white splotch against the dark recess of the sheltering cavern near the top of the rim. The little 4-4-0 with the passenger train is Denver & Rio Grande's No. 100, a Baldwin product of 1881 named the HESPERIS. Motive power of the Santa Fe Southern Railroad acquired by the Denver & Rio Grande included two Pittsburgh 2-6-0 types, No's. 3 and 4; these Moguls reportedly were built for the Cairo & St. Louis Railroad as No's. 26 and 27, later being assigned D&RG numbers 24 and 25. They were the second engines to display this road number, the original No. 24, the MOSCA, and No. 25, the HARDSCRABBLE, having been disposed of before the Santa Fe Southern was acquired by the Rio Grande.

(Wm. H. Jackson collection, courtesy of State Historical Society of Colorado)

MASON MACHINE & LOCOMOTIVE WORKS turned out four locomotives of the 2-8-6T type for the Denver, South Park & Pacific in 1880. These engines were No. 25, the ALPINE, No. 26, the RICO, No. 27, the ROARING FORK, and No. 28, the DENVER, shown here at the factory. They had 36 inch drivers, 15 x 20 inch cylinders, and weighed 55,340 on their driving wheels. The crews on the South Park liked the Mason engines for their free steaming qualities and the accessibility of the Walschaert valve gear.

DENVER, SOUTH PARK & PACIFIC RAILROAD, operating a narrow gauge system in the heart of the Rockies, used a number of William Mason's locomotives designed for heavy service on steep grades and sharp curves. Shown here at the Mason factory is No. 4, named the SAN JUAN. Along with her sister, No 3, the ORO CITY, this 2-6-6T type was built in 1878 and had 13 x 16 inch cylinders, 37 inch drivers, and weighed 43,850 pounds on her drivers. The SAN JUAN later became No. 41 on the Denver, Leadville & Gunnison Railway and was scrapped in 1889.

WILLIAM HENRY JACKSON'S camera captured this majestic scene of Colorado mountain railroading between Nathrop and Mt. Princeton Hot Springs. Engine 42 and coach 9 of the old Denver, South Park & Pacific Railroad are shown in the boulder-strewn valley of Chalk Creek Canon; in the background you can see the sheer chalk cliffs that gave the locality its name. The peak at upper right, scarred with the avalanche run where winter snowslides roared down, is Mount Princeton, one of the chain of Colorado peaks named for famous colleges. Actually, Chalk Cliffs are not a true chalk formation, but a deposit of decomposed feldspar mixed with a clayish substance. Engine 42 of the South Park was a 2-8-0 built by Cooke in 1883, Shop No. 1479. She had 15 x 18 inch cylinders, 36 inch drivers, and her weight on drivers was listed at 62,900 pounds The little mountain hog was scrapped in 1916, after having been renumbered Denver, Leadville & Gunnison 199 in 1889 and finally Colorado & Southern 38 in 1898. (Courtesy of State Historical Society of Colorado)

SOUTH PARK HOG, old No. 51 was a 2-8-0 built by Baldwin in 1880. The Consolidation type had 37 inch drivers, 15 x 18 inch cylinders, and a stack that dwarfed her boiler. Renumbered 191 under the Denver, Leadville & Gunnison operations, she later became No. 31 on the Colorado & Southern and reportedly was disposed of to a lumber company prior to 1902. This view shows No. 51 on a freight train at The Palisades, a sheer bluff on the upper bend of the Sherrod Curve, located between Woodstock and Alpine, Colorado, near the famous Alpine Tunnel which pierced the summit of the Continental Divide at an elevation of 11,605 feet.

GRACEFUL CONSOLIDATION TYPE on the old South Park was No. 63, built by the Cooke Locomotive & Machine Works in 1883, Shop No. 1498. The big "Boo Hoo" stack was typical of much of the South Park's motive power. Her 36 inch drivers, powered by 15 x 18 inch cylinders, permitted her boiler to set low on the frame, giving the engine a low center of gravity. Note the main air reservoir mounted at the rear of the tank. This engine became Denver, Leadville & Gunnison No. 212, later Colorado & Southern No. 51, and was cut up in 1920.

THE DENVER, SOUTH PARK & PACIFIC threaded three-foot gauge rails over some of the toughest terrain the Rockies had to offer, with five locations topping the 11,000 ft. elevation marks and grades that ran over 4 per cent. To handle the passenger and freight trains over these incredible grades and sharp curves the road operated a large stud of 2-8-0 and 2-6-0 locomotives with low drivers that made them especially suited for the back-breaking work. Engine 71 was a sturdy Cooke 2-6-0 outshopped in 1884, bearing Shop No. 1554. The little mountain climber had 40 inch drivers, 14½ x 18 inch cylinders, and an ample dome to carry her sand supply. Numbered 113 on the successor Denver, Leadville & Gunnison Railway, she ended her days as Colorado & Southern's No. 8, scrapped in 1938.

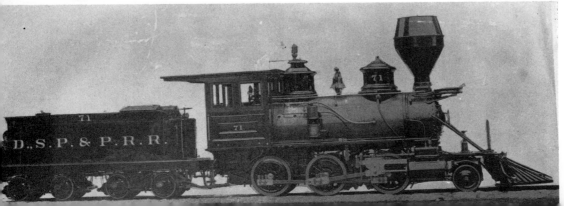

A TRESPASSING COW came to a sad end at Idaho Springs, Colorado, on July 29, 1899. The bovine, partly visible here beneath the leading tender trucks, came to her untimely parting at the wheels of Colorado & Southern Railway's Engine 6, a 2-6-0 built by Cooke in 1884. Originally No. 69 of the old Denver, South Park & Pacific, she later bore No. 111 on the Denver, Leadville & Gunnison roster before the lines were acquired by the Colorado & Southern Railway.

(Collection of Dr. S. R. Wood)

SOUTH PARK MOGUL, Engine 35 bore the name, DILLON, in honor of the Colorado village located beyond Breckenridge, north of Boreas Pass. Built in 1882, she was a Brooks product with 38 inch drivers and 15 x 18 inch cylinders. The poor steaming qualities of the Brooks engines caused the South Park crews to term them "ice cream freezers." The DILLON became Denver, Leadville & Gunnison No. 162, was rebuilt with a new boiler in 1894, became Colorado & Southern No. 22, and was scrapped in 1927.

MINOR DIFFICULTIES of mountain railroading are depicted in this view taken near Lawson, Colorado, on March 6, 1899. Engine No. 13, a narrow gauge Cooke Mogul of 1884 vintage, piled into a snow slide and hit the ties, coming to a precarious halt with her pilot overhanging the rock embankment along the frozen waters of Clear Creek. Workmen are busily shoring her up with a cribbing of hewn ties preparatory to re-railing her. No. 13 was originally the Colorado Central's No. 15, later operated by the Union Pacific, Denver & Gulf, and became No. 13 of the Colorado & Southern in 1898. The Mogul at left serving as a relief engine is her sister, C&S No. 12, formerly Colorado Central's No. 14. Both engines had 14½ x 18 inch cylinders and 40 inch drivers, and bore Cooke Shop No's. 1558 and 1559 when they rolled out of the factory in February, 1884.

(Collection of Dr. S. R. Wood)

THE LOOP, GEORGETOWN

GEORGETOWN, BRECKENRIDGE & LEADVILLE RAILROAD was faced with a problem in engineering when the tracks were laid from the end of the Colorado Central Railroad at Georgetown up the canyon of Clear Creek to Bakerville (now Graymont), Colorado. To the north towered Silver Plume Mountain and the rocky battlements of Leavenworth Mountain rose to the south. The direct distance from Georgetown to Silver Plume is slightly over 2 miles, but the difference in elevation is 638 feet. Built in a straight line, the road would have had a grade of over 300 feet to the mile, so the locating engineers laid out a series of loops, one crossing over itself, and reduced the grade to 143 feet per mile; the distance traversed by this line was extended to 4.47 miles, in order to obtain the easier grade. This William H. Jackson photo shows the famed Loop, looking east down Clear Creek Canyon. West of where this view was taken, the line made two tight reverse curves and crossed Clear Creek twice in the process; the passenger train in the foreground is bound down-grade, and in the middle distance an engine can be seen headed uphill, standing on the high bridge. The track winds down the slope at left, crosses Clear Creek on the truss bridge seen over the baggage car of the passenger train, then follows the stream down the right bank, passing under the high steel span supporting the light engine; beyond the toe of the ridge at right, the grade swung over to South Clear Creek and ran on to Georgetown.

(Wm. H. Jackson photo,

135

DEVIL'S GATE BRIDGE was a famous railroad structure that formed a part of the noted Georgetown Loop, located on the Georgetown, Breckenridge & Leadville Railroad. This W. H. Jackson view, taken about 1901, shows a passenger train on the spidery span, hauled by Colorado & Southern Eng. No. 8, a 2-6-0 Cooke of 1884 that was originally Denver, South Park & Pacific No. 71. The construction of the bridge, 300 feet long, was commenced in 1882 and was carried out by the Phoenix Bridge Company. The first locomotive rolled across the completed span on February 28th, 1884, with Engineer George Cooper at the throttle. The bridge had an 18 degree, 30 minute curve and stood on granite piers quarried in the vicinity; the rails on the span were over 95 feet above the channel of Clear Creek, the brawling mountain stream alongside the lower tracks of the famed spiral segment of the narrow gauge railroad.

(W. H. Jackson, photo, courtesy Denver Public Library Western Collection)

DENVER PACIFIC RAILWAY was a standard gauge line extending 106 miles between Denver City, Colorado, and Cheyenne, Wyoming Territory. It was constructed under a charter of the Union Pacific, Eastern Division, Railway, the road that later emerged as the Kansas Pacific. The Denver Pacific was opened for traffic on June 23, 1870, and was operated under the control of the Kansas Pacific. This photo shows one of the line's Baldwin eight-wheelers with the first train into Greeley, Colorado.

(Courtesy of Denver Public Library's Western Collection)

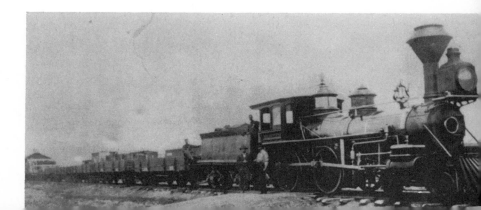

DENVER PACIFIC RAILWAY photographs are collector's items, with only a scattered few known to exist. This copy of an old half-tone engraving shows Denver Pacific's Engine No. 4, an American Standard named the WALTER S. CHEESMAN in honor of one of the directors of the road residing in St. Louis, Missouri. In the 1870's, the road was under the guidance of President D. M. Edgerton, General Manager Robert E. Carr, and General Superintendent T. F. Oakes. Mr. C. W. Fisher was Asst. Superintendent and John McKenzie held the position of Master of Machinery.

(Courtesy of Denver Public Library's Western Collection)

COLORADO CENTRAL originally assigned this McQueen 4-4-0 their road number 7, but this photo taken in Denver about 1885 shows her bearing the Union Pacific's No. 585 when she was on the roster of that road's subsidiary Union Pacific, Denver & Gulf. The Colorado Central name is visible on the wooden cab panel. Note the huge Congdon stack and the metal sheathing on the wooden stave pilot. The locomotive had 62 inch drivers and 17 x 24 inch cylinders, but no record is available regarding her final disposition.   (Courtesy of Union Pacific Railroad)

DENVER, LEADVILLE & GUNNISON's Engine 109 is halted at Roscoe, Colorado, with a railroad employees excursion train on the Clear Creek Canyon line in 1898.

WRECK NEAR GOLDEN, COLORADO, on the old Colorado Central line; Denver, Leadville & Gunnison's Eng. 108 and two cars of Train 53 are overturned on the creek bank. Engine 198 and way car at left, with Mogul 154 and a work train outfit at right.

COLORADO CENTRAL RAILROAD mixed train, headed by Engine 155, is posed in typical Colorado locale; a stream winds through the rocky canyon, with mines and ore reduction mills along the tracks. Rich shipments of ore rolled over the crooked rails of many Colorado lines.

UNION PACIFIC, DENVER & GULF Engine 7, a Cooke 2-6-0 built in 1884 and formerly Colorado Central No. 14, heads a slim gauge Silver Plume-Denver varnish, Train 52, at Empire, Colorado, on the Clear Creek line in 1894. The town was located at some distance from the railroad station. Note the open platform passenger equipment.

(All photos, collection of Dr. S. R. Wood)

COLORADO MIDLAND RAILROAD was incorporated in 1883 for the purpose of constructing a standard gauge line from Colorado Springs, Colorado, to Salt Lake City, Utah. Guided by J. J. Hagerman, the road started construction at a connection with the Santa Fe at Colorado Springs in 1886 and by 1887 was completed to Glenwood Springs. With the assistance of some joint construction with the Denver & Rio Grande, the line reached Grand Junction in 1890 and terminated there. Financial reverses threw the road into receivership, but the final blow fell in 1918 when the road was ordered closed by the United States Railroad Administration. The section from Colorado Springs to Divide was resurrected as the Midland Terminal Railway. The famous Colorado Midland route over Hagerman Pass had been abandoned in 1899, eliminated by use of the Busk Tunnel. The glorious memories of the road are recaptured in this view of a Colorado Midland varnish, hauled by No. 25, a 4-6-0, at Glenwood Springs. The photo was probably taken after the 1897 receivership, as the emblem on the tender uses the designation, "Railway," rather than the former "Railroad."

(Courtesy of Denver Public Library, Western Collection)

MANITOU & PIKES PEAK RAILWAY, although only 8.9 miles in length, was one of the best known short lines in the West. The road was chartered in November, 1888, and the track was completed from Manitou, Colorado, to the summit of Pike's Peak and placed in operation on June 30, 1891. The road was built as a scenic railway and the extreme grades, 8 to 25 per cent, made the use of a rack-rail necessary. More familiarly known as a cog railway, the track consisted of three rails, the center one having notches cut into its running surface; a driving wheel operating on this rack rail had cogs or teeth cut into it which meshed with the notches in the rack rail, providing the necessary adhesion to permit the engine to climb the steep ascent. The first engine built by Baldwin for the Manitou & Pike's Peak Railway in 1890 was a four-cylinder compound, featuring the Abt System of gearing. The Abt rack-rail engine, weighing 52,680 pounds, was capable of pushing 25,000 pounds up the maximum grades, the cars being shoved up ahead of the engines; the locomotives were not turned, but backed down grade with the cars trailing them. An unusual feature was the boiler design, placed at an angle on the frame; when the engine was standing on the level, the butt of the boiler was elevated, giving it a tilted look, but when the engine hit the steep pulls, the boiler became nearly level. The MANITOU, shown here, was one of the later Abt System engines and bore Baldwin Shop No. 10919. Water was carried in the side tanks and fuel in the rear bunker.

(Wm. H. Jackson Collection, courtesy of State Historical Society of Colorado)

139

COLORADO MIDLAND RAILROAD'S Engine 53 was a Consolidation built by Baldwin in 1897, bearing **Shop No. 15134.** Note the extended piston rods and the triangle emblem bearing the legend, "PIKE'S PEAK ROUTE."

COLORADO MIDLAND RAILWAY Engine 201 was a compound Consolidation turned out by Baldwin in 1901, bearing Shop No. 18631. Note the change in the style of lettering and numbers as compared with the photo at the top of this page. (Both photos, Collection of Dr. S. R. Wood)

COLORADO MIDLAND RAILROAD acquired three locomotives which were used in the construction of the first section of the line west from Colorado Springs. Pictured here is the Midland's Engine No. 2, a cap-stacked Consolidation with a wagon-top boiler and spoked tank wheels. No. 2 was built by the Schenectady Works in 1886, Construction No. 2226, and had 20 x 24 inch cylinders, 52 inch drivers, and a working boiler pressure of 160 lbs. per square inch. The Colorado Midland established a yard and engine facilities at Colorado City, three miles west of Colorado Springs, and the road's early activities centered around this terminal. The Midland route, much of it through boulder-strewn mountains, was costly to build, since it included a great deal of construction through solid rock. The second tunnel, located near Manitou, contained a "blowout," a pocket of scoria, volcanic ash, and plumbago. The plumbago was a substance similar to graphite and coated men and tools with a film so slippery that Contractor James H. Kyner's crew had to keep kegs of sand available, using it to apply on their hands and the handles of their picks and sledge hammers. Branches of the Midland were built from Arkansas Junction to Leadville, Basalt to Aspen, and from Cardiff to Spring Gulch, the latter known as the Jerome Park Branch. Basalt was the scene of a great tragedy on the Midland, long remembered by railroaders throughout the West. The road operated Saturday excursion trains from the Aspen mining community to the Glenwood Springs; patronized largely by women and children, these excursions were called the "laundry trains," the passengers going to the famous Glenwood Springs to swim in the pool there. While one of these specials was halted at Basalt, a helper engine left unattended on a spur moved out toward the main line, probably activated by a leaky throttle. It sideswiped the loaded coaches, breaking off the boiler check valve and allowing a scalding stream of steam and hot water to blast into the cars. The result was a horror that the passage of time can never erase.

FLORENCE & CRIPPLE CREEK RAILROAD a colorful Colorado mining road, purchased this sturdy 4-6-0 from Schenectady in 1900. She was numbered 23 and named the GRANITE, and is shown here heading a combine and a coach. The engine had 42 inch drivers, 16 x 20 inch cylinders, and weighed 87,400 pounds. The GRANITE was later sold west, and became No. 23 of the narrow gauge Nevada-California-Oregon Railway. She was scrapped at Sparks, Nevada, in 1927, one year before the N-C-O was taken over by the Southern Pacific.

Atchison, Topeka & Santa Fe's 895, a Dickson 2-6-0 built in 1897, was photographed by Fred Jukes at Colorado Springs in 1898. She had 19½ x 28 inch cylinders and 73 inch drivers.
(Courtesy of Fred Jukes)

. . . A Bouquet Of Colorado

Colorado & Southern Engine 13 was a 2-6-0 built by Cooke in 1884, and was originally Colorado Central No. 15; she served on the Union Pacific, Denver & Gulf before acquiring the Colorado & Southern numbering in 1898.
(Collection of Dr. S. R. Wood)

Florence & Cripple Creek Railroad's No. 23 was named GRANITE and was a 4-6-0 built by Schenectady in 1900; she was later sold to the Nevada-California-Oregon Ry., along with her sister, Engine 22, named the VINDICATOR.
(Collection of Dr. S. R. Wood)

Colorado Midland's Engine 15 was a trim 4-6-0 with a cap stack. When the Midland was torn up in 1918, a similar ten-wheeler, No. 36, was sold to the California Western R.R. & Nav. Co.; another Midland engine went to Oregon's Gales Creek & Wilson River R.R.
(Denver Public Library's Western Collection)

Mountain Climbers . . .

Colorado Midland's Engine 29 was a 4-6-0 built by Baldwin in 1888 bearing Shop No. 9206. The vertical cylinder under the cab is the main reservoir for storing air produced by the "one-lung" pump.
(Collection of Dr. S. R. Wood)

Argentine Central Railroad, a narrow gauge mining pike, ran from Silver Plume to Waldorf, Colorado, 16 miles. Built by E. J. Wilcox to serve his mine, it used geared engines such as Shay No. 4. The road was completed in 1906 and scrapped in 1919.

(L. C. McClure photo, collection of Dr. S. R. Wood)

MONTANA SMASH took place near Bearmouth, west of Drummond, on the main line of the Northern Pacific on March 5, 1905. This bad head-on collision was caused by a misunderstanding of train orders by the crew on Extra 1252 East, an unscheduled freight train. This crew erroneously believed they had a "run late" order stating that Train No. 3, the westbound passenger, was 3 hours 20 minutes late on her timetable schedule; actually, No. 3 was only 20 minutes late, and the mistake ended in this pile-up. The photo was taken shortly after the crash and shows smoke still wisping from the stack of each engine. Engine 1252 was a tandem compound Consolidation type, her double cylinder showing clearly; note the badly kinked main rod on Engine 1322, just to the right of the white-clad cook, and the fact that all of the driving wheels of both locomotives came to rest hanging in the air, clear of the rails. The telescoped Railway Post Office car jammed over No. 3's engine gives mute testimony to the force of the collision. Wrecks such as this one pressured the railroads to install automatic block signals to prevent similar accidents and cut down the toll of dead and injured passengers and crewmen. The development and use of such safety devices was instrumental in building the wonderful safety records enjoyed by modern railroads.

(Courtesy of Ronald V. Nixon)

MONTANA CENTRAL RAILWAY was organized in 1886 and operated about 249 miles of standard gauge lines, the main stem running from Great Falls to Butte, via Helena. From Great Falls the road swung southwest and followed along the upper reaches of the Missouri River, passing east of the main divide of the Rockies and west of the Big Belt Mountains. A branch running southeast out of Great Falls divided into smaller branches tapping the mines at Sand Coulee, Stockett, and Neihart. The main line and most of the branches were opened for service between 1887 and 1893, the branch from Lewis Junction to Stockett being opened in 1898. Main traffic over the road was coal and ore, with seasonal livestock movements. The Sand Coulee coal was perhaps the most notorious locomotive fuel ever to land on the grates of an engine. The Great Northern Railway, controlling the entire stock of the Montana Central, extended a line from the southeastern branch out of Great Falls through the Judith Gap to Billings and a connection with the Burlington's line from Nebraska, the latter coming from Edgemont, North Dakota, through Sheridan, Wyoming. A branch from the Great Falls-Billings line extends from Moccasin to Lewiston, Montana. This early Montana Central passenger train is posed against the rocky terrain so typical of the intermountain region; the lever at right on the coach platform is a part of the old Miller "hook" coupling device.

(Courtesy of Great Northern Railway

GREAT NORTHERN RAILWAY, completed through to Puget Sound in 1893, set about to capture some of the lucrative traffic that had formerly rolled over the lines of the Northern Pacific. Between Helena and Boulder, Montana, on the Great Northern's road from Great Falls to Butte, the Hill trackage intersected the Northern Pacific's Elkhorn Branch. This interesting photo, taken about 1900, shows a Northern Pacific passenger train headed by a 4-4-0 at upper left, on a stone-piered steel girder bridge over one of the numerous streams that sparkle through the mountains of western Montana. At lower right, a Great Northern 2-6-0 drawing a combination baggage car and coach passes under the Northern Pacific tracks. In line with the Hill policy of branch lines and feeder connections, the Great Northern purchased the old Great Falls & Canada Railway in northern Montana and in 1903 conveyed it to the affiliated Montana & Great Northern Railway. The Great Falls & Canada Railway was built as a narrow gauge line and extended from Great Falls to Sweet Grass, Montana, thence across the Canadian line to Lethbridge, North West Territory (now Alberta Province), Canada. The Montana section of the road was broadened to standard gauge in 1902 and was 134 miles long; the section of the line in Canada, about 67 miles in length, passed to the Alberta Railway & Coal Company and later to the Canadian Pacific Railway.

(Courtesy of Ronald V. Nixon)

MOUNTAIN MELODRAMA was enacted on the Northern Pacific's line near Dorsey, Idaho, about 1903. Engines 79 and 396 were pushing a rotary snowplow ahead of them as they fought their way over the rugged branch that threaded the Bitter Root and the Coeur d'Alene ranges. Crossing the famous "S" trestle, the train, which consisted of local passenger equipment in addition to the rotary plow, was forced to a halt by a big snowslide that covered the track ahead. Shortly after the train stopped, a second slide buried the rails on the opposite end of the trestle, marooning the train. Before the crews could dig their way clear, a third avalanche swept down the gorge and carried away most of the "S" trestle, so named from its shape. A helper locomotive and a caboose at the rear of the train were carried down with the crashing structure, leaving the coach at right balanced in a precarious angle high above the canyon. Occupants of the car tilted so dangerously all crawled to safety through the car ahead, and tradition says that one hardy soul returned to the dangling coach to retrieve a pair of rubbers he had left behind in the rush to a safer location. (Barnard photo, courtesy of Ronald Nixon)

UTAH WESTERN RAILROAD started life as the Salt Lake, Sevier Valley & Pioche Railroad, a narrow gauge line projected by Generals P. E. Connor and E. M. Barnum to run from Salt Lake City to the mining region around Pioche, Nevada. Grading started in 1872, but the company failed and work was suspended in 1873 after some 20 miles of rough grading had been accomplished. Construction was resumed on June 15, 1874, when John W. Young and other Mormon investors from Salt Lake City organized the Utah Western Railroad to take over the franchise of the Salt Lake, Sevier Valley & Pioche. The road was completed from Salt Lake City to Stockton, in Tooele County, Utah, a distance of about 40 miles, early in 1875. The noted Salt Lake photographer, C. R. Savage, took this photo of Engine No. 2, the EDWARD HUNTER, at Point of the Mountain, Utah; Engineer Evan Jones is shown oiling around the 3 foot gauge Mogul while workmen load ballast on flat cars and two combines loaded with passengers stand in the background. In 1881 the Utah & Nevada Railway, owned by the Union Pacific, took over the Utah Western and its four locomotives. The line later became part of the Oregon Short Line & Utah Northern system, controlled by the Union Pacific. (C. R. Savage photo, courtesy of Arthur Petersen)

By Pacific Shores.

Intelligent leaders of our American government, sparked by the visionaries of the day, took the first steps toward making a transcontinental railway become a reality by ordering a series of surveys across the vast reaches of the West. The military men who laid out these original routes proved the possibilities of rail lines to the Pacific Ocean, but the sturdy pioneer settlers did not wait for the Iron Horse to come to them.

"RAILROADING IN A BARN" is how the boomers described operations on the old Central Pacific's transcontinental route over the Sierra Nevada of eastern California. The problem of snow on the line in the high mountain passes confronted many Western railways, but the Central Pacific set out to lick Old King Winter shortly after they had completed the road in 1869. Since the snowplows in use at the time were inadequate to handle the deep drifts, the management set crews to work building a roof over the track to keep the snow off. These snowsheds, or "galleries," w e r e constructed of both sawed timber and log uprights, sheathed with rough planks designed to shelter the tracks. By 1873 the road had more than 30 miles of covered track and at one time this figure increased to 60 miles, but improved snowplows outmoded them. This early Central Pacific view shows the main line roofed over at Norden, the summit of the Sierras; the cupola-topped building at right is a covered turntable and adjoining it is an enginehouse, helper locomotives being turned at this point. Norden is located at an elevation of 6.880 feet; in the winter of 1880, the station recorded a total snowfall of 783 inches, or 65¼ feet, which is ample snow for any man's railroad!

(Courtesy of Southern Pacific)

Railroading gained an early foothold in the region between the Rockies and the Pacific Ocean and the settlers in the area were quick to realize the advantages of this form of transport. Short lines were built in California, the Sacramento Valley Railroad putting its first locomotive into operation in 1855, and soon the light iron of the Central Pacific was climbing the rocky flanks of the Sierra Nevada in the race east to meet the Union Pacific.

In 1865 the San Francisco firm of H. J. Booth & Company, also known as the Union Iron Works, was turning out locomotives that compared very favorably with the products of the old established Eastern manufacturers. Even earlier, the Vulcan Iron Works of San Francisco had turned out some primitive locomotives for the portage railroads operating around the Cascades in the Columbia River in Oregon and the Puget Sound area around Seattle soon heard the rumble of cars on the short tram road serving the coal mines there.

The Pacific West proved to be one of the great treasure chests of the United States. The timber, seemingly endless in extent, grew to dimensions that awed the pine loggers from Maine and the Great Lakes. Gold, silver, copper, and coal were to be found in hoards undreamed of, and in later years the earth poured forth a wealth of oil. Rich grazing lands supported countless herds of sheep and cattle, and the

virgin soil produced bumper crops of grain, fruit, and vegetables. Even the arid desert regions were turned into fertile croplands following the introduction of irrigation. Small wonder that farmers from the drought-blasted, grasshopper-plagued Great Plains were attracted to the Pacific slopes; no cyclones carried away their barns and dwellings, and the gentle rains assured them ample moisture for the tender crops.

Blessed by the environment, agriculture and manufacturing were rapidly developed to a high degree and an ever-expanding network of rails were built to handle the commodities. These railroads ranged from the frugal, farmer-built pikes with wooden rails to elaborate systems financed by the wealth of California's mines and the silver treasures of Nevada's Comstock Lode.

Unique among the early railways was the Sonoma Valley Prismoidal Railway, built north from Norfolk, California, in 1876. This odd road was designed to operate on a single rail laid atop a wooden base or prism, rollers bearing on the sides of the prism balancing the rolling stock. The prismoidal road was the invention of an Alabama man named Crew, and was promoted in California by Joseph S. Kohn. A locomotive for this strange "one-legged" railroad was built by the Pacific Foundry in San Francisco, and about 3 miles of road was actually constructed.

GRANT LOCOMOTIVE WORKS turned out two 4-6-0 type engines for the Central Pacific Railroad in 1867. These were given road numbers 48 and 49 and were named the TOIYABE and the TOQUIMA. In the 1880's, General Master Mechanic Andrew J. Stevens rebuilt these tenwheelers to 4-4-0 types and No. 48 is shown here after that conversion. She has been equipped with Stevens' famed "monkey motion" valve gear and cylinders, and a typical "duck-tail" cab with large clerestory and an overhung deck roof to shelter the fireboy as he palmed wood into her firebox. This engine was renumbered 1366 but was declared uneconomical and was written off the books as scrapped at West Oakland on August 28, 1899. Louis Stein donated the old glass plate negative of this view to the Railway & Locomotive Historical Society in 1958.   (Courtesy of Ben W. Griffiths)

Trial trips were made and the engine and cars ran smoothly, but no practical solution was found for grade crossings over the prismoidal trackage and the project soon folded up. The Sonoma Valley Railroad, a narrow gauge line of standard design, grew out of the ruins of the defunct prismoidal road and was eventually extended to Sonoma; the sole locomotive of Kohn's odd line became a stationary engine at Shellville.

The steep grades on Pacific slope logging lines gave birth to another unique type of steam locomotion. This contraption was the Fouts Grip Wheel, known to Northwest loggers as the "walking Dudley." A vertical boiler mounted on a small car furnished the power for this device, which propelled itself along by means of a road cable extending the length of the road. This cable was passed around a grip wheel to provide the necessary traction, and logs were skidded along the track between the rails. The Fouts Wheel was installed on the logging show of Henry Colvin at Marshland, on the lower Columbia River, and was a decided improvement over the bull teams formerly used on the skid roads. The first Fouts machine used by Colvin was left unattended at the top of a grade and it ran away, leaping into a canyon, but was salvaged and rebuilt, giving many years of satisfactory service.

Those ubiquitous geared locomotives, the Shay, Climax, and Heisler, found wide acceptance in the Pacific region. Sidewinders blasted their rapid exhaust from the Idaho pine to the California redwoods, snaking logs out of the tall and uncut. Geared locomotives served the steep grades of mining pikes, in addition to laboring for the loggers, and some were destined to play more glamorous roles, such as the geared pots that hauled passengers up the slopes of California's Mount Tamalpais.

The terrain of the Pacific West set the stage for a great deal of colorful and spectacular railroading. In the high passes of the mountains, snowsheds housed miles of track and spidery bridges spanned the awesome canyons. The flat desert regions were natural racetracks, and some ballast-scorching runs were made on these long level tangents. The story of Walter "Death Valley" Scott and his Coyote Special, operated over the Santa Fe, is well known to all railroad enthusiasts, but the stories of many other speedy runs are buried in ancient train dispatchers' sheets and in the memories of rail veterans.

Engineer Joe Callicot rose to local fame in 1872 when he rushed the Salem, Oregon, fire department to Portland to combat a blaze that nearly wiped out the business district. His woodburning Oregon & California eightwheeler roared over the newly-completed track at such dizzy speeds that upon arrival in East Portland, the horses brought along to draw the equipment were in an uncontrollable frenzy and the steam pumper had to be muscled aboard the Willamette River ferry by a gang of men in order to convey it across the stream to the scene of the fire.

When a similar conflagration threatened to

devour the wooden structures of pioneer Seattle, a Northern Pacfic crew from Tacoma rushed firemen to battle the blaze behind a funnel-stacked 4-4-0 in record time.

The silk and tea express trains running east from Pacific Coast ports operated on schedules that rivalled those of the fastest passenger trains of the day and added a colorful chapter to the rail lore of the region.

In addition to the daily movement of passengers and freight, the railroads offered numerous humanitarian services. The earthquake and fire that struck San Francisco disrupted rail service around the Bay area, but the ashes were still smouldering when the trains were put back into operation. Solid trains of food, tents, medicines, and other commodities donated for the relief of the inhabitants left homeless by the disaster were rushed by rail to the stricken city.

Shortly after the turn of the century, the big German bark MIMI blundered onto the sand spit at the mouth of Oregon's Nehalem River, coming to rest high and dry in an upright position. When efforts were made to refloat the vessel, she capsized in the boiling surf beyond reach of the helpless watchers on the beach.

In response to the appeal for help, the Pacific Railway & Navigation Company sent a locomotive and car on an errand of mercy. This special ran to the Coast Guard Station at Barview and loaded aboard the Lyle gun used to shoot lines to stranded vessels, then hurried along the rails bordering the ocean to the point nearest the wreck. The lifesaving crew and equipment were hurried to the beach, but were unable to shoot a line to the unfortunate survivors clinging to the exposed portions of the capsized ship. Captain and his surfboat crew finally reached the wreck and saved several survivors, but 17 men lost their lives in the tragedy.

The Northwestern Pacific Railroad was also involved in a marine disaster. In December of 1916, the United States Navy's submarine H-3 ran aground on the northern coast of California, stranding on Samoa Beach four miles north of Humboldt Bay. The Coast Guard crew from Humboldt Station rescued the crew of the helpless submersible and the Navy set about to salvage the craft. The huge armoured cruiser, USS MILWAUKEE, was sent to the scene early in January, 1917, to attempt to tow the submarine off the beach, but a hawser parted under the strain and the mighty MILWAUKEE herself veered onto the beach and was stranded. Her crew was evacuated by breeches buoy but the 9,700 ton cruiser was a hopeless loss. Salvage

efforts were implemented when a spur track on a trestle was built from the nearby Northwestern Pacific line out to the stranded vessel. Ironically, the submarine was later salvaged by means of a channel cut through the sands and the vessel was floated into the calm waters of Humboldt Bay.

The railroaders of the Pacific region were a resourceful lot, ready to meet any emergency that arose. Floods, forest fires, and other disasters were taken in stride and the crews kept the trains rolling whenever it was humanly possible to do so. The Southern Pacific's great struggle to conquer the flooding Colorado River when it threatened to inundate the Imperial Valley is but one of many examples of the fortitude of Western railways. From the initial break-through in 1905 until the river was at last sealed off in February, 1907, men and machines fought the encroaching waters; the estimated cost of licking the unruly stream was set at about $4,000,000.

Huge projects or simple problems, the rails tackled them with a will. One Oregon logging line was plagued by derailments of a vexing nature. Cars loaded with fir logs would jump the track and run along the roadbed for great distances before they would finally drop off the ends of the ties and break the train in two. This was a costly business, as the derailed cars ruined the ties they ran on and often sheared off the bolts holding the angle bars in place. A trainmaster came up with an ingenious solution to end this problem. At intervals along the line he had pits dug between the rails and the gauge of the track at these points widened slightly. If a car was derailed, it did not travel far until it fell into one of these pits, breaking the train in two and halting the damage to the track.

The great snow blockade that choked the mountains of the West in the winter of 1889-90 proved the mettle of railroad men and officials alike. The high passes were blocked by huge walls of snow, defying the efforts of snow crews to open the lines. Train No. 15, the OREGON EXPRESS, was bound from Sacramento to Portland when the January blizzard of 1890 struck. The train, with Charles Crocker's private car, MISHAWAUKA, tied on the rear end, beat north as far as Tunnel 11 in the Sacramento River canyon before stalling in the drifts. For over sixty hours the snow fell in sheets, until it lay eight feet deep on the level. Food for the passengers on the marooned train ran low, and the crew carried in supplies from Sims, the nearest station, located a mile and one half back

LARGEST FERRY IN THE WORLD was the claim made for the SOLANO, built by the Central Pacific Railroad in 1879. The big wooden sidewheeler was slightly over 420 feet long, 116 feet wide, and over 18 feet in depth. She was a double-ender type, with a dual set of controls and two pilothouses, enabling her to operate without turning, the pilot simply changing from one wheelhouse to the other. Each big paddlewheel was powered by a single cylinder measuring 60 x 132 inches, connected to a walking beam, and steam for these two huge cylinders was supplied by 8 boilers of the old Scotch marine design. The SOLANO began operations on December 28, 1879, ferrying Central Pacific trains across Carquinez Straits, the narrows between Suisun and San Pablo bays, where the waters of the Sacramento and San Joaquin rivers flow down to San Francisco Bay. This 1889 view was taken at Port Costa, the landing on the south shore opposite the north bank terminus of Benecia, California. This ferry service provided a short cut for trains bound from the Bay area to Sacramento, eliminating the original route through Niles Canyon and Stockton. A diamond stack 4-4-0 is shown heading a train of "duck-bill" roofed varnish off the decks of the big paddler. A second huge train ferry, the CONTRA COSTA, joined the SOLANO in 1914, built by the Southern Pacific. This historic ferry service ended on October 15, 1930, when the Southern Pacific opened the Martinez-Benecia bridge over the waters of Suisun Bay.
(Courtesy of Southern Pacific)

down the canyon. A relief crew from Dunsmuir attempted to reach the stalled EXPRESS but got only as far as Castle Crag, and a relief train from Sacramento hit a work train in the drifts above Redding, delaying their rescue attempt.

Twelve feet of snow buried the mountain terminal located at Dunsmuir, and a slide north of Upper Soda Springs buried the Dunsmuir snowplow and a locomotive, further hampering efforts to open the line. It was not until January 20th that a relief train from the south reached Sims. Aboard were about 300 men, working stiffs and riffraff recruited to help dig out the blocked tracks, and these men had been without food for more than thirty hours as they toiled through the frigid drifts with pick and shovel.

Hungry and nearly frozen, they rebelled when they reached Sims and demanded food. They stormed the depot where Assistant Superintendent Pratt and other officials had sought refuge and were placated only when the brass hats arranged to have some milk cows butchered; the strikers ravenously devoured the meat raw and then resumed their strenuous labors. The Southern Pacfic's snowbound PORTLAND EXPRESS was liberated and left Sims to return to the safety of Sacramento on January 22nd, having been marooned in the snowy canyon since January 15th.

Al F. Zimmerman, a Union Pacific locomotive engineer currently holding an official position with the Brotherhood of Locomotive Engineers, presented the writer with a manuscript that tells the story of the Western railroad man. Scrawled in pencil, the brief memoirs of nearly 49 years of railroading on the former Oregon

151

Railway & Navigation Company's lines were recorded in 1929 by George L. Mans, a retiring locomotive engineer. The spelling is crude and phonetic, but the experiences and feelings of this veteran merit recording exactly as he jotted them down; the only liberty taken by the writer has been to interpret a few passages and these interpretations are enclosed in parenthesis. Here is the first-hand account of one of the courageous railroaders who helped open the American West:

"A Rambling Storey of My Life of nearly 49 years of Service with the Oregon-Washington Railroad & Navigation Co."

"I left the Central Pacific in Nevada in the Spring of 1880, where I was firing a 17 x 24 Rogers on No. 1 and 2, passenger, between Wadsworth, Nevada, and Truckee, California. I was started on this wild goose chase by a old man working in the roundhouse at Wadsworth. He in turn got his idea from a book published in Portland, Or., called the West Shore. (The old WEST SHORE magazine.) They were booming Walla Walla (Washington) at that time. Walla Walla valley was suposed to be virtuly vackent, Lots of game & fish and a wounderful Stock countrey all waiting to bee taken up. So we started to this Land of promis. We were 60 days on the road from Wadsworth to Walla Walla. We had everyting a man would nead (in) a wild sunsettled countrey, Blak Smith & carpenter tooles, medison, clothsing, provesions, 5 gals. of Best whiskey, a fine Rifel, fishing tackle, in fact we had most everything in that wagon that wasent locked up or nailed down. Our trip was very plesent, good weather all the way and fine fead for our horses, Lots of game and fish.

In those days it was Washington Teritorey, you could take up a home Sted, a timber culture & premsion (Pre-emption), 180 acors in all, so we expected to settle in the hart of Walla Walla Valley, build our Log cabin on the cornor of the 2 home Steds. We were going in the Stock Business. Dad Mathuse (Matthews?), my partnor, had about twentey thousand dollers, I had a little money, a good rifel & lots of Ambish. But a lass, Our castle blue up. I took sick in Pendleton (Oregon) and when we got up on the divide between Pendleton & Walla Walla you could look all over the valley, just one wheat field after a nother. Some one beat us to it. Rit there I lost all confidance in Books & things you see in print. Well, I kept my

trunk and went to a cheap hotell. Dad Mathus wanted to go on up to the Paluce (Palouse) countrey so I gave him all but my trunk. I expected to folow later. They sent me to the hospital & when I came out I was broke, they robed my trunk at the hotell so all I had was the same outfit I had camped out in & Roughed it in for 60 days and not any money to get a stamp to write home and a mung Straingers, you say, was I home Sick, oh boy. Well, about then my Life took a turn. When I got able I got a job for a short time in a warehouse then I got firening a little Narow gague Eng. out of Walla Walla (On the old Walla Walla & Columbia River Railroad). The day I hired out at Whitman, 5 miles west of Walla Walla, met my future wife.

All the road they had at that time was to Wallula from Walla Walla, conected with the Steam Boat (The steamers ran on the Columbia River). I halled all the tyes that built the road from Wallula to Cyote (Coyote), from Milton, all heued tyes. The company then quit building from that end & made a Standard gauge of it from Portland, it at one time was intended to bee all narow gague. (This was the Oregon Railway & Navigation Co. line.) I pulled the first train that ever went into Umatilla & the last narow gague Engine out of there. Umatilla was quite a town at one time. Wife & I spent our huney moon there, we wer happey & conted (contented), mabey because we dident no any better. Since then I have had a verid experiance. I have worked about all over the Road, pulled every thing from a work train to the Presedent. Bucked Snow out of La Grande (Oregon), winter of '86 & '87, with a blind plow, Long hours, wet, sleapey, Sometimes hungrey & half frose. I took some aufl rides down that Mountain on boath sides, the faster you went the better work you did, to throw the Snow a way from the track. If we had ever hit a rock, a tree, or a broken rail we would bee going yet.

I was in a reck east of the The Dalles in the sand (The winds up the Columbia Gorge drifted blow sand onto the tracks in this area; the district was called "The Sandy" by the oldtimers), Engine turned over & crippled my back so I gave up the main line work for a Switch Eng. I made 2 trips to Portland on passenger before there was any (railroad) bridge, took passengers a cross (the Willamett) on a ferry, turn table was B.O. (Bad Order, i.e., out of service) at The Dalles, we had to run clear through.

And now, Dear Friends & Brothers, as I am

COMMUTER TRAIN MOTIVE POWER requisites were responsible for the unusual class of locomotives represented here. The morning and evening rush of local passenger traffic out of Oakland, California, prompted the Central Pacific's officials to seek an engine to handle these trains with efficiency and dispatch, and the problem was handed to Master Mechanic A. J. Stevens. Under his supervision, the Sacramento Shops turned out 7 engines of this type, the first one bearing Shop No. 13 and the other 6 bearing consecutive shop numbers. First of the lot, No. 230 on the Central Pacific roster, was completed in 1881 and her 6 sisters were finished in 1882. Several novel features were included in their design; a 2-6-2 tank type, they carried their coal and water in bunker and tank on the frame, to give added weight on the drivers and increase their traction for fast starts. These engines incorporated a novel brake, probably designed by Chief Draftsman George A. Stoddard, which was operated by foot by the engine crew. A pedal was connected to rods and counter-weights, exerting sufficient braking power on the brake shoes; a portion of this device can be seen between the main and rear drivers. The tank engines had 16 x 24 inch cylinders, 48 inch driving wheels, weighed 44 tons, (51½ tons loaded with fuel and water), carried 1,600 gallons of water in the side tank, and the bunker at the rear held 4 tons of coal. They were designed to operate in either direction with equal facility, eliminating the need for turning them, hence the stave pilots located on both ends. No. 236, shown here, ended her days as the Portland Div. shop engine.

(Courtesy of David L. Joslyn)

drawin near to the End of my Last Run, I want to thank you one and all for the little acts of kindness I have receved at youer hands. Allso thank the O-W.R.&N. for the many acts of kindness to me and mine, But in Return, to the Co. I can consciencely say I have been a faithful Survent to them. I thank God for his protection during these many years.

George L. Mans

When Engineer Mans wrote the foregoing, he summed up the inner feelings of Western railroaders. Trusting in Divine Providence, they built the West and truly earned the accolade of "faithful Survent."

EXPERIMENTAL LOCOMOTIVE proved to be the forerunner of a long-lived series of 4-8-0 engines in service on the Central Pacific and the Southern Pacific. Built in the Company's shops at Sacramento, California, in 1882 under the direction of the noted General Master Mechanic Andrew J. Stevens, the engine was assigned Central Pacific No. 229 and incorporated many advanced features. She was equipped with Stevens' double valves, activated by three eccentrics on each side and operated by a power reverse gear consisting of a curved rocker and two reverse levers. Other novel features included clasp driver brakes, a combustion chamber built into the boiler ahead of the firebox, and an air compressor mounted under the fireman's side of the cab. The cab itself was of unusual design, featuring a large clerestory and a "duck-tail" overhang to shelter the fireman when that worthy was busy on the deck. Her large diamond stack was designed for either wood or coal burning operations, but the Central Pacific boys neglected to check clearances and when No. 229 rolled out of the shops in April, 1882, this big stack failed to clear the door, knocking the stack off and damaging the top of the shop doorway. The engine proved so successful on the Sierra Nevada grades that she and some of the men who helped build her were sent East to the Cooke Locomotive Works, where 20 engines of the same style were constructed, with a few minor changes. After several renumberings, the old 229 ended her days in 1935 as Southern Pacific's 2925. Others of this type were in use as late as the 1950's, mostly relegated to service on the branch lines of Southern Pacific's Portland Division. They were a familiar sight in western Oregon, churning across the Coast Range and struggling up the Santiam Canyon in their battle with the grades of the Cascade Mountains on the Mill City Branch. From an original glass plate owned by the Pacific Coast Chapter of the Railway & Locomotive Historical Society.   (Courtesy of Ben W. Griffiths)

SIDE-DOOR CABOOSE No. 45 was a typical freight hack in use before the turn of the century on the Central Pacific. Note the big "possum belly" under the car for storing tools and gear.
          (Courtesy of Association of American Railroads)

HEADED FOR THE GOLDEN GATE, the old Overland Limited of the Southern Pacific stands ready to leave the yards in Ogden, Utah, about 1892. Train, engine, and dining car crew help the photographer record the scene for posterity; the gent in the white shirt and vest, indicated by the inverted arrow, is William John Lee, the Ogden yardmaster. Engine 265 was a coalburning 4-4-0 equipped with A. J. Stevens' monkey motion valve gear; she was built by the Central Pacific in the Sacramento Shops in 1888, Shop No. 56. Later renumbered Southern Pacific's 1420, she was scrapped in 1911.
(Courtesy of Arthur Petersen)

BUSY JUNCTION POINT on the Southern Pacific was Lathrop, California, where the line through the San Joaquin Valley to Bakersfield and points south left the old main stem from Sacramento to San Francisco Bay. This 1891 view shows the wooden roundhouse at Lathrop and a sextet of locomotives being groomed for their daily stint. The number of the engine at the far left is not discernible, but next in line is Southern Pacific's No. 324, a 4-6-0 built by Cooke in 1888 and shown here with a straight shot stack; the number on the next engine to the right is too dim to permit positive identification; next in line is No. 152, a Schenectady 4-6-0 built in 1882 as No. 72 of the Southern Pacific Railroad of Arizona; the next engine, sporting a footboard which indicates yard service, is the 1509, a 4-6-0 built by Wm. Mason in 1864 as the 6-spot engine of the Central Pacific; the engine in the last stall at the right is No. 221, a 4-4-0 built in the Central Pacific Shops at Sacramento in 1887. Notice the old harp type switch stand used to operate the stub switch in the right foreground.
(Courtesy of Southern Pacific)

DAWN OF A NEW ERA was recorded around 1890 when the camera caught the image of the first Southern Pacific freight train to be equipped with Westinghouse automatic air brakes. The automatic air brake was a wonderful improvement over the old "straight air" brake, causing an automatic application on both sections of a train that broke in two. With the former air brake such an accident not only failed to halt the rear portion of a parted train, but also caused the loss of brakes on the forward section, contributing to many accidents. The 4-4-0 handling this experimental train was Southern Pacific's Engine 380, a coal burner built by Schenectady in 1889.　　　　(Courtesy of Southern Pacific)

NEVADA-CALIFORNIA-OREGON RAILWAY was formed by the Moran Brothers of New York in 1888 to take over the operations of the 3 foot gauge Nevada & California Railroad, successor to the Nevada & Oregon Railroad; the latter concern was incorporated in 1881 to take over the paper-stage project of the Western Nevada Railroad, a dormant outfit formed in 1879 to build a railroad from Wadsworth, Nevada, to Walker Lake and Bodie. The first Nevada & Oregon Railroad was started in 1880 and graded a few miles from Reno; the second company of this name took over the work in 1881 and 31 miles in operation from Reno to Onieda by the fall of 1882. Under Moran operations, the road reached Hackstaff in 1889, and was completed into Amadee, Calif., in 1890; it was extended to Termo in 1900, the Madeline in 1902, reached Alturas in 1908 and was completed into the Lakeview, Oregon, terminus in January, 1912. Engine No. 3 of the N-C-O was named the ERASMUS GEST, a 4-4-0 built by Baldwin in 1887, Shop No. 8791. The 3-footer carried her main reservoir atop her boiler and sported a diminutive pilot plow; her cylinders were 12 x 18 inches and she wheeled along the Goose Lake line on 42 inch drivers. When the Southern Pacific acquired the N-C-O in 1928, she was stored at Sparks, Nevada, and was scrapped in 1938. One of her builder's badge plates is a treasured possession of Prof. S. R. Wood.　　　　Collection of Dr. S. R. Wood)

Central Pacific 130, the FAVORITE, was a McKay & Aldus 4-4-0 built in 1868. She appears here in front of the El Capitan Hotel in Merced, California.
(Courtesy of David L. Joslyn)

. . . A Treasure Of Steam

Central Pacific 210, a 4-6-0 built by Cooke in 1876, poses with a work train on the trestle at Yuma, Arizona, in 1887.
(Courtesy of G. M. Best)

Locomotives Of The Far West . . .

Southern Pacific 270, a 4-4-0 built in the Sacramento Shops in 1888, stands on the sage-covered flats of Winnemucca, Nevada, in 1889; crew shown are Engineer John Smith and Fireman W. E. Cobb.
(Courtesy of David L. Joslyn)

Central Pacific 237, the famous EL GOBERNADOR, at Sumner (Bakersfield) California in 1884. The huge 4-10-0 was built in the Central Pacific's Sacramento Shops in 1883, Shop No. 21.

Central Pacific 1799 was a neat 4-6-0 built by Cooke in 1893, Shop No. 2272, and later became Southern Pacific's 2226. She is posed here at the Sacramento train-shed in 1896.

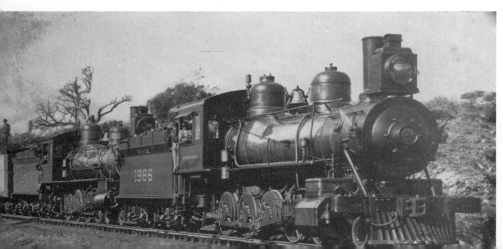

A brace of Southern Pacific 4-8-0's ready to tackle the steep Tehachapi grade near Mojave, California, in 1897. Leading engine 1986, a Schenectady cross-compound, was built in 1891 and was later Southern Pacific 2932, scrapped in 1949; the 1984, behind, was a simple Cooke built in 1882 as S.P. 78, scrapped in 1950 as No. 2931. (Three photos, Collection of G. M. Best)

Trio of Central Pacific-Southern Pacific 4-4-0's turned out in the Sacramento Shops by General Master Mechanic A. J. Stevens and Chief Draftsman George A. Stoddard. Upper view shows 2nd 122 of the C.P., Shop No. 26, built in 1886 with outside engine truck bearings. Center is C.P.'s 3rd No. 166, Shop No. 29; built in 1886, she was later S.P.'s 1365. Lower photo shows S.P. 217, Shop No. 42, built in 1887 and renumbered 1414. All were fitted with "monkey motion" valve gear and had sandboxes located under their boilers.

(All from glass plates owned by Pacific Coast Chapter, Railway & Locomotive Historical Society, courtesy of Ben W. Griffiths)

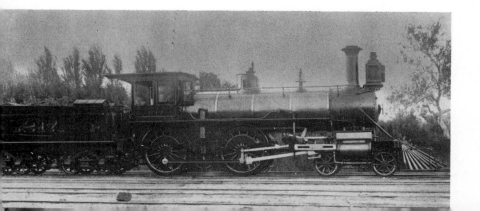

San Francisco & North Pacific Railroad's No. 3, the W. C. RALSTON, was built in 1870 by H. J. Booth & Co. (Union Iron Works) of San Francisco, Shop No. 15, and later became Northwestern Pacific's second No. 7, retired in 1920. She was a 4-4-0 woodburner.
(Collection of Dr. S. R. Wood)

Southern Pacific's 292 was a pretty 4-6-0 built by Rhode Island in 1888, Shop No. 1963. She ended her days as S.P. 2184, and was once assigned to the Shasta Division in northern California. She had 18 x 24 inch cylinders and 57 inch drivers.
(Courtesy of Ben W. Griffiths)

John Souther's Globe Loco. Works, South Boston, Mass., built this woodburning 4-4-0 in 1868 for the Oregon Central R.R. and she was named the UMPQUA. On her way to Oregon, she was re-sold to the Central Pacific as their No. 124, later 1212. In 1900 she was sold to Folsom Prison, where this photo was taken before scrapping in 1906.

Seattle, Lake Shore & Eastern Engine 8 was a 2-8-0 built by Richmond in 1895, Shop No. 2496. She became Seattle & International's No. 8, then Northern Pacific 47 and was rebuilt to an 0-8-0 type.
(Collection of Dr. S. R. Wood)

Central Pacific 240 was a 4-6-0 built in the Sacramento Shops in 1888, Shop No. 32. Renumbered S.P. 2196, she served on the lines in Oregon before being scrapped in 1912. (Pacific Coast Chapter, R&LHS negative, courtesy of Ben W. Griffiths)

Oregon & California Railroad's 1244 was formerly No. 6, the ALBANY, and was built by Baldwin in 1870. Cylinder on running board near cab generated carbide gas for the headlight, replacing the original oil lamp; prudent firemen aired the lamp-house before attempting to light the jet, to prevent explosions of accumulated gas
(Courtesy of Eugene Register-Guard)

CARSON & COLORADO RAILWAY was incorporated in 1880 and constructed a 3 foot gauge line from Mound House, Nevada, to Keeler, California. The 299 miles of narrow gauge iron connecting these two terminals was driven to completion by 1883. At Mound House, the road connected with the storied Virginia & Truckee Railroad, serving the rich Comstock Lode region. The Carson & Colorado, financed by Darius Ogden Mills, was intended to run to the Colorado River but after passing along the eastern side of historic Walker Lake, the course was changed and the line swung southwest into the Candelaria mining region. Crossing Montgomery summit in the White Mountains, the little pike crossed into California and meandered down through Owenyo to a terminus at Keeler, on the east side of Owens Lake. West of Owenyo towered Mt. Whitney and across the Panamint Range to the east lay the desolate wastes of Death Valley. In viewing the completed line, D. O. Mills reportedly stated that "either this line was built 300 miles too long or 300 years too soon!" Sporadic mining booms kept the road operating and in 1905 it was absorbed by the Nevada & California Railway, becoming a branch of the Southern Pacific in 1912. Engine No. 2, the BODIE, was Baldwin's Shop No. 5430, a trim 4-4-0 built in 1881 with 41 inch drivers and 14 x 18 inch cylinders; she was scrapped in 1907. This photo was taken by F. Gutekunst, a professional photographer of Philadelphia who was engaged by the Baldwin Loco. Works.

(Courtesy of Fred Jukes)

NARROW GAUGE ENGINES OF THE NORTH PACIFIC COAST RAILROAD

No. 2, the SAN RAFAEL, was nicknamed JACKRABBIT. Built by Mason, Shop No. 537, in 1874, she was an 0-4-4-F type with 12 x 16 inch cylinders and 44 inch drivers. No. 3, the TOMALES, a 4-4-0 built by Baldwin in 1875, Shop No. 3722, had 12 x 16 inch cylinders and 42 inch drivers. The NPC ran from Sausalito to Cazadero, California, with a branch from San Anselmo to San Rafael and San Quentin, on San Francisco Bay.

No. 8, the BULLY BOY, a Mason 0-6-6F, built under Shop No. 584 in 1877, ready to leave Sausalito with a Mill Valley train; the ferry SAUSALITO is moored in the left background. The North Pacific Coast Railroad later became part of the Northwestern Pacific.

(All photos, courtesy of Roy D. Graves)

TIDEWATER TERMINAL, this view taken about 1910 shows the sprawling roundhouse facilities of the **Southern Pacific** located at West Oakland, California, on the shores of San Francisco Bay. American Standard and 4-6-0 locomotives dominate the scene, with one of the old 2900 class 4-8-0's visible at left.

(J. A. Casoly collection, courtesy of Ben W. Griffiths)

WET RAILROADING! Two employees wade ahead of a passenger train on the inundated tracks of the Southern Pacific during the floods of 1905-06 in the Imperial Valley of California. The great Colorado River sent its waters sweeping into the Salton Sink, forcing the Southern Pacific to relocate the railroad several times before the break was finally sealed. The main line shown here has a breakwater of sand bags to protect the track from the gnawing currents. The man at left, in vest and striped shirt, may be John Tangney, the fighting roadmaster who led his crews in the memorable battle against the floodwaters that threatened to wipe out the Imperial Valley.

PARK & OCEAN RAILROAD was a standard gauge line organized around 1879 by a group of San Franciscans that included such notables as Leland Stanford, Chas. Crocker, and C. P. Huntington. The line was opened for service about 1883 and ran from a transfer point on the Haight Street cable car line out present Lincoln Way to 48th Avenue and Balboa Street, near the beach. The first motive power reportedly was of the steam dummy type, but the road later operated several saddletankers, such as the 6-Spot, shown here with a string of open-sided cars and her proud crew. Engine No. 6 was a Baldwin product, a 2-4-2 tank type, and showered cinders over many car-loads of delighted excursionists, the Park & Ocean enjoying a lucrative traffic of pleasure-seekers bound for the attractions of the beach.

(Courtesy of Ronnie Hughes)

TEHACHAPI LOOP, one of the wonders of Western railroading, is shown in this 1876 photograph. The American Standard heading the 5-car varnish on the upper level of track is Central Pacific's No. 222, fresh from the Schenectady works with builder's number 1002 on her plates; on the lower level, foreground, stands Central Pacific's No. 108, a Rogers 4-4-0 built in 1868 and named the STAGER. Sister engines on the C.P. from Rogers' plant bore such names as RUNNER, RUSHER, RAMBLER, ROLLER, PACER, and COURSER. The loop was laid out by William Hood, Asst. Chief Engineer under the noted Samuel S. Montague, and carried the CP-SP rails out of the San Joaquin Valley over the Tehachapi Mountains. Tunnel No. 9, shown here, was one of 18 tunnels bored in the conquest of the Tehachapi, armies of Chinese laborers doing most of the pick and shovel work.

(Courtesy of Southern Pacific)

HIGH STREET STATION in Alameda, California, forms the setting for this view of a narrow gauge varnish on the old South Pacific Coast Railroad shortly after the line was opened for through traffic to Santa Cruz. The woodburning 4-4-0 standing in front of the diminutive wooden frame depot is one of the American Standards built new for the road by the Baldwin Locomotive Works. Her crew, left to right, includes Engineer George Clark, Fireman Dan Quill (seated in the cab), Brakeman Jimmy Kelly, and Conductor Thomas H. David.   (Courtesy of Southern Pacific)

UTAH SOUTHERN RAILROAD, a standard gauge line organized in January, 1871, had 12 locomotives on its roster when it was merged with the Utah Central Railroad and the Utah Southern Extension Railroad in 1881, forming the Utah Central Railway. Utah Southern Railroad Engine 5, a Schenectady 4-4-0, was built in 1880 and after consolidation is reported to have been renumbered Utah Central Railway's No. 11. Pictured here as she originally appeared, she stands on the turntable in front of Milford, Utah's sturdy brick roundhouse.   (Don Roberts collection, courtesy of Herb Arey)

"THE SANTA FE OVERLAND ON THE DESERT" was the original caption applied to this Wm. H. Jackson photograph, reproduced here from a badly cracked glass plate negative. The speedy 4-6-0 wheeling the wooden passenger cars is Engine 56 of the Southern California Railway, a Santa Fe subsidiary that took over considerable trackage in California in 1889. Included in the Southern California Railway operations were the lines built in 1887 by the California Central from San Bernardino to Duarte and the San Bernardino-Barstow line, opened in 1885 by the California Southern. While Jackson left no definite identification regarding the exact location of this view, it was probably taken out on the Mojave Desert between Victorville and Barstow; note the gnarled Joshua trees at the left, struggling for existence in the arid, sandy soil. The extreme heat that scorched the Mojave-Barstow-Needles region seared the souls of railroaders who toiled in the sun-baked desert and a steady stream of boomers flowed through the terminals, pausing only long enough to make a short stake before drifting to more agreeable climes.

(Wm. H. Jackson collection, courtesy of State Historical Society of Colorado)

KASLO & SLOCAN RAILWAY was one of the roads backed by Jim Hill's Great Northern to tap the mining regions of British Columbia, extending 28.8 miles from Kaslo to Sandon, B.C., with a 3 mile spur from Sandon to Cody. Chartered in 1892, the 3 foot gauge line was placed in operation from Kaslo, on Kootenay Lake, to the zinc, lead, and silver mine area around Sandon in November, 1895. In 1899 the road became part of the Kootenay Railway & Navigation Company, a British firm controlled by the Great Northern. Avalanches and forest fires plagued the line, business fell off, and in 1912 the road was acquired by the Canadian Pacific, converted to standard gauge, and joined with the former Nakusp & Slocan Railway. This photo shows narrow gauge Engine No. 2 at Kaslo, near the foot of the switchback leading up the Kaslo River canyon; the 2-Spot and her sister 2-6-0, No. 1, were Baldwin woodburners acquired from the Alberta Railway & Coal Company. (Courtesy of British Columbia Provincial Archives)

THE OLD WEDGE SNOWPLOWS often proved ineffective when winter blizzards piled the drifted snow across the rail lines of the West, and railroaders welcomed the new rotary type snow plows. These devices eliminated the earlier and extremely hazardous methods of bucking snow, a procedure that sent many a railroad man to glory and an early grave. A great competitive trial was held on the Alpine Pass line of the Denver, South Park & Pacific near Hancock, Colorado, in April of 1880, the conventional rotary proving its superiority over an auger-shaped Centrifugal Snow Excavator designed by Mr. Orange Jull and built by the Rogers Locomotive Works. Shown here is Northern Pacific's rotary plow No. 6, handled by Engine 97 at Wallace, Idaho, about 1902.

(Courtesy of Ronald V. Nixon)

INFORMAL OPERATIONS of many Western short lines are reflected in this old train order from the narrow gauge Walla Walla & Columbia River Railroad, the famous "Rawhide Railroad" built by Dr. Dorsey S. Baker between Walla Walla and Wallula, in eastern Washington. Dated at Walla Walla, Washington Territory, October 7, 1880, the order reads: M. M. Weekes, Conductor, and Geo. Manns, Engineer: Tomorrow morning Oct. 8th after No. 6 west bound passes Junction you will take seven or eight Freight cars with Glenns crew and proceed to Gid Cummings wheat pile and have loaded with wheat keep'ng clear of all regular Trains. After loaded put the mon mill spur. 12 (indicating the end of the order). This primitive operating order was issued by J. M. Hill over the signature of H. W. Fairweather, Vice President and General Superintendent of the road. In its infancy, the railroad had but limited warehouse facilities and farmers in the rich wheat land piled their grain at convenient points along the track for shipment to the steamboat terminus at Wallula.

(Courtesy of Al Zimmerman)

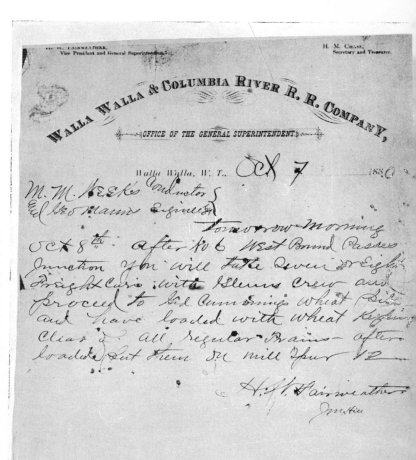

TACOMA EASTERN RAILROAD, incorporated in 1890, was a logging line that ended up as a branch of the Chicago, Milwaukee, St. Paul & Pacific. Headquarters for the road were located in Bismarck, Washington, a suburb of Tacoma, and by 1903 the standard gauge pike had been opened from the terminus to Eatonville, 32 miles. The road served numerous large sawmills and logging camps located around Tanwax and Kapowsin and was eventually extended to Ashford, with branches to Elbe and Morton. In addition to logs and lumber, the road had quite a thriving passenger business. Ashford, near the base of Mt. Rainier, was the nearest rail terminal to that scenic peak and around 1905 a giant outing of mountain climbers from all over the country saw 3,000 people pour into the tiny station in 36 hours, handled by 13 special trains. In the early days of operations, wrecks and runaways were not infrequent on the mountain pike, and the camera of the late John C. Ashford, veteran locomotive engineer and railroad enthusiast, recorded this pile-up of Tacoma Eastern's Engine 5 in 1910. Henry Clay French, boomer railroader on many Western pikes, served as a conductor on this road under General Manager John Bagley; French's engineer was Walter Dorn, a skilled runner who eased the log trains over the rough and crooked track when the line was first placed in operation. By 1905 the road had 9 locomotives on its roster ,with geared engines operating on some of the logging spur lines.   (Courtesy of Fred Jukes)

NORTHERN PACIFIC'S ENGINE 28, her tender stacked high with wood, posed for this photo outside the old stone roundhouse at Claymont, Minnesota, in 1884. Engineer George H. Daimond stands in the gangway of the 4-4-0 and Fireman Arthur Clark is seated at the left cab window.   (Courtesy of Ronald V. Nixon)

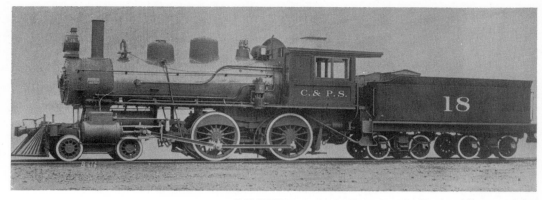

COLUMBIA & PUGET SOUND'S Engine 18 was a trim
4-4-0 built by the American Locomotive Company for the
Washington coal hauler. Note her main reservoir located
under the boiler behind the cylinder saddle.
(Collection of Dr. S. R. Wood)

CHICAGO, MILWAUKEE & PUGET SOUND was formed to handle the Pacific Coast extension of the Chicago, Milwaukee
& St. Paul Railway, later consolidated under the corporate title of Chicago, Milwaukee, St. Paul & Pacific Railroad. Fortunately for railroad historians and those who love the steam power of a by-gone era, many Western communities were
blessed with men who combined their affection for the locomotive with their skillful photographic abiilty. One of these
devoted artisans operating in the Pacific Northwest, Dr. J. Foster Adams, produced this excellent shot of Engine 3509
of the Chicago, Milwaukee & Puget Sound. The high-stepping Baldwin Atlantic displays what was the acme of passenger
power shortly after the turn of the century, when lanky 4-4-2's blasted along the transcontinental routes with their brigades
of light-weight wooden passenger cars. No. 3509 exhibits a rather unusual mechanical combination, the application of
Walschaert valve gear to an engine equipped with Vauclain compound cylinders.
(J. Foster Adams photograph, courtesy of Fred Jukes)

MEMORIES OF THE OLD WEST are recalled by this photograph taken at Pocatello, Idaho, in the late 1880's. Grouped around Union Pacific's Engine 699 are shop and engine men, while two blanket-draped Indians stand on the pilot beam. The 4-4-0 was built by the New York Loco. Wks., Rome, New York, in 1888. (Courtesy of Arthur Petersen)

An Album
of Western Railroads.

VARNISHED CARS of the Northern Pacific a r e depicted at the Livingston, Montana, station in this 1890 photograph. The trim 4-6-0 heading the passenger train is Northern Pacific's No. 442, a coal burner with a stave p i l o t and spoked e n g i n e t r u c k wheels.   (Courtesy of Ronald V. Nixon)

MASON & OCEANA RAILROAD was a narrow gauge logging pike 40 miles long, running out of Buttersville, Michigan. Chartered in August, 1886, the 3 foot trackage was opened to Stetson in 1888, extended to Goodrich in 1901, and reached Maple, Michigan, in June of 1903. In 1905 the road had 5 locomotives on its roster and was under control of President M. F. Butters. Engines 5 and 7 were 2-8-0 types built by the Grant Loco. Works; No. 5, upper, is coupled to a passenger coach and displays an assortment of gear suspended from hooks on her tank, including a "goose-neck" link for couplings between high and low draw-heads. The 5-Spot was built in 1881, while No. 7, lower, was built in 1882. The 2-Spot on the Mason & Oceana was a Shay built by Lima, Shop No. 154. (Both photos, Collection of Dr. S. R. Wood)

ELECTRIC STREET RAILWAYS spelled the end of many of steam-operated city and suburban street railroads in the United States, and the colorful little steam locomotives used in this type of service faded into oblivion. Not all of them went straight to the junk yards when the trolley cars took over, however. A prime example of conversion to other service is the little 2-6-0 tank type shown here, trailing two sets of disconnected bunks loaded with fir logs. This engine was originally a steam dummy type, Baldwin's Shop No. 10683, and was operated on the old Willamette Bridge Railway lines in Portland, Oregon, as their No. 4. When her days of pulling street cars were over, she was sold to the Star Logging & Lumber Co. at Rainier, Oregon, and was placed in service on their logging road. The dummy body that had enclosed her boiler when she was used on the street railway was partially removed, only the rear portion being left to serve as a cab. The logging road later became the Yeon & Pelton property, and the little ex-dummy served them faithfully. Note the construction of the bridge and roadbed shown here; logs have been laid upon other logs to carry the ties and rails across the low ground and the small stream, eliminating expensive earthwork and bridging.

(Courtesy of Oregon Historical Society)

LOGGING RAILROAD INCLINE (Opposite Page) may have been inspired by the inclined planes used by several pioneer rail lines in the East, a notable example being the Old Allegheny Portage Railroad with its ten inclines. The steep incline shown here in a photograph from the Yeon collection in the files of the Oregon Historical Society is reported to be the first of its kind used in the Pacific Northwest. The three cars loaded with logs are being lowered down the terrific grade to the booming and rafting grounds on the lower Columbia River in Oregon. The cable attached to the cars is being controlled by a steam donkey engine, located out of sight at the upper end of the incline; cables bound each load of logs onto the incline cars to keep them from plunging off on the perpendicular descent. Conductor H. L. McAdams, a retired Espee railroader, once witnessed a runaway on one of these steep inclines; the cable holding the cars broke and they came down the hill with a roar, struck an oil tank car on the bottom end of the spur and shot on out into the timber, demolishing themselves and the tank in their wild flight. Some of these inclines were long and elaborate, with a counter-balance system and a passing track located midway up the hill, permitting loads to descend while a cut of empties were being hauled back upgrade.

(Yeon Collection, courtesy of Oregon Historical Society)

PENINSULAR RAILWAY'S No. 3, at work in the timber of western Washington, was a Baldwin 4-6-0 built in 1890 as the No. 3 of the Satsop Railroad, where she was named WM. SHORTER.
(Collection of Dr. S. R. Wood)

WOODBURNING PRAIRIE TYPE, No. 7 of the Wisconsin Logging & Timber Co. was a sturdy Baldwin, shown here at a log dump near Oak Point, Washington. Her owners formerly logged in Wisconsin before following the timber trail to the Pacific Northwest.
(Courtesy of Ben Baldridge)

HUMBOLDT & MAD RIVER No. 1, the ADVANCE, was built by Baldwin in 1875 and hauled giant redwoods on John Vance's logging road in northern California. This 0-4-0 saddle tank later became No. 1 on the Eureka & Klamath River.
(Collection of Dr. S. R. Wood)

HINCKLEY & COMPANY of San Francisco, also known as the Fulton Iron Works, built this 0-4-0 with pannier tanks for Flanagan & Mann's Newport Coal Co. at Marshfield, Oregon, in 1872. After hauling coal from the old Libby Mine, the engine is shown here logging in Blossom Gulch, on Coos Bay.
(Courtesy of Jack Slattery)

NATIVE DAUGHTER OF THE BEAR STATE, this rare old photo shows Engine No. 3 of the Arcata & Mad River Railroad, the NORTH FORK. Originally an 0-4-4 tank type rebuilt to an 0-4-2 with a tender, she was constructed in San Francisco, California, about 1883 by the Golden State & Miners Iron Works. The NORTH FORK served for many years on the Redwood Coast pike, being renumbered in 1903 as the A&MR 2 and was scrapped in 1932. The Arcata & Mad River was organized late in 1881 and built 14 miles of track from Arcata Wharf to Korbel, California. By 1893 another 17 miles of track was in operation from Korbel to and along the waters of the Mad River. Although the narrow gauge road was primarily used to haul redwood, the line also offered some passenger service and several lives were lost when a passenger train fell through the bridge over Warren Creek in 1896. The original of this photograph is owned by Everett L. De Golyer, Jr., of Dallas, Texas, and was copied by Dr. S. R. Wood.
(Collection of Dr. S. R. Wood)

REDWOOD LOGGING ALONG GUALALA RIVER was carried on by the Gualala Mill Company, operating in Mendocino County, California, south along the coast from the old redwood operations in Humboldt County. George Webber and John Rutherford erected a redwood sawmill at Gualala in the early days, and in 1868 they sold one-half interest in their operations to William Heywood and S. H. Harmon. By 1872 they had opened a logging railroad from the mill to Burns Landing, some 2½ miles to the south. The original line was a tram road, built to broad gauge to permit horses or oxen to haul the cars loaded with the huge redwood logs. As the timber was cut off, the railroad was extended further into the forest, and locomotives were acquired to replace the four-footed motive power. Engine 3 of the Gualala Mill Company, pictured here, was an 0-4-0 woodburner built by Baldwin in January, 1886. She bore Baldwin's Shop No. 7677, had a sunflower stack with a screen spark arrester, and carried her wood and water on a four-wheel tender. The longhandled reverse lever, or Johnson bar, can be seen on its quadrant through the open front cab door. (Collection of Dr. S. R. Wood)

OREGON RAILWAY & NAVIGATION CO. used this Baldwin saddle tanker as a switch engine at The Dalles, Oregon, in the 1880's. Built in 1882 as the OR&N's No. 52, she later served as a shop engine at the Albina, Oregon, terminal.
(Courtesy of Don H. Roberts)

NARROW GAUGE DINKY, this Baldwin-built 0-4-2 served the iron works located at Oswego, Oregon. Note the third rail trackages leading to the Southern Pacific interchange and the crude screen spark arrester on this iron colt.
(Courtesy of H. H. Arey)

THE WOOD TRAIN, long neglected by rail historians, played a humble but vital role in railroading, collecting fuel wood from trackside points and delivering it to terminals and fueling stations. Canadian Pacific's Engine 217 is shown here with a wood train; the 4-4-0 was built by Brooks in 1873 for the United States Rolling Stock Co., became Canada Central Ry. No. 17, then CPR 217 before this photo was taken in 1887.

THE WORK TRAIN served an important position in railroad construction and maintenance. Here Engine 13 of the narrow gauge South Pacific Coast poses with the railroad's pile driver. The locomotive was a husky 2-8-0 built by Baldwin.

UNION PACIFIC DEPOT at Rawlins, Wyoming, was a good example of the larger stations built by pioneer Western roads. Such structures frequently housed dining rooms, baggage facilities, and division offices, in addition to the waiting room for passengers and the regular telegraph office. Note the assortment of frontier characters in this 1868 view of Rawlins station.

(Courtesy of Union Pacific Railroad)

IN PRE-ATOMIC DAYS the Oregon Short Line depot at Arco, Idaho, presented this quiet scene. Engine 525, a 4-6-0 with an auxiliary water tank, heads up a mixed train before the wooden station, while the windmill at left pumps the station's water supply. The scenery is typical of the arid portions of the West, with sagebrush slopes running up to the rimrock.

(Courtesy of Arthur Petersen)

OREGON SHORT LINE'S Engine 1, a 2-6-0 with diamond stack, is shown here on the narrow gauge trackage at Salt Lake City about 1900. The slim gauge pike, extending to a terminus near Stockton, Utah, was torn up after completion of the Leamington cut-off from Salt Lake to a junction near Lynndyl about 1902. (Courtesy of Arthur Petersen)

TYPICAL OLDTIME DEPOT was this station building on the Illinois Central at Fonda, Iowa. Located between Iowa Falls and Sioux City, the wooden structure boasted a pump and well, at left, and a train order signal with a white lens for "Clear" position. Signs in this 1894 view indicate the depot housed the agencies of the Western Union Telegraph and the American Express.

(Courtesy of Illinois Central Railroad)

BURLINGTON, CEDAR RAPIDS & MINNESOTA RAILROAD was organized in 1868, completed from Burlington to Plymouth, Iowa, in 1873, and after a receivership, emerged in 1876 as the Burlington, Cedar Rapids & Northern Railway. The locomotive JOHN H. DAVEY of the old BCR&M, a 4-4-0 built by Hinkley & Williams, is shown here at Cedar Rapids, Iowa, in 1870.

(Courtesy of Bernard Corbin)

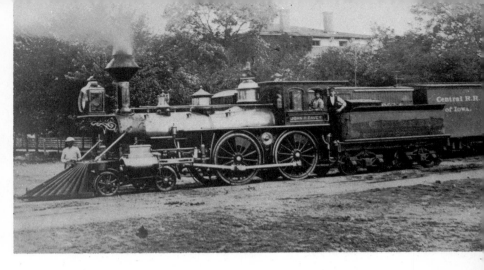

CORVALLIS & EASTERN'S No. 4 was built by Cooke in 1886 for the Oregon Pacific Railroad, successor to the Willamette Valley & Coast. She later was acquired by the Southern Pacific and renumbered 1302.

(Arey photo, author's collection)

RIO GRANDE SOUTHERN's No. 9, a Baldwin Consolidation, is shown here in the Colorado mountains. She was built in 1881, Shop No. 5800, as No. 249 of the Denver & Rio Grande.

(Collection of Dr. S. R. Wood)

CHICAGO, BURLINGTON & QUINCY No. 170 was a diamond stack 4-4-0 built in 1871 by the Manchester Locomotive Works, Shop No. 312.
(Collection of Dr. S. R. Wood)

KEARNEY & BLACK HILLS Engine No. 2 and her train at the Sumner, Nebraska, station in 1894, year of the ill-fated A.R.U. strike. This Nebraska short line became a Union Pacific branch from Kearney to Callaway, later extended to Stapleton.

CHICAGO & NORTH WESTERN'S Engine 38 was built in their own shops in October, 1879. Note the eagle on her bell and the solid deck metal plate covering the entire turntable pit.
(Collection of Dr. S. R. Wood)

CHICAGO, DUBUQUE & MINNESOTA R.R. was opened between Dubuque, Iowa, and La Crescent, Minnesota, in 1871; a branch from Turkey River to Elkport, Iowa, gave the line a total of 134 miles of track. Eng. 22, the DUBUQUE, was a 4-4-0 built by Hinkley in 1871.

MISSOURI, IOWA & NEBRASKA R.R. was chartered in 1870 and by 1871 was in operation from Alexandria, Mo., to Centreville, Iowa. Eng. 7, the CLARK, was Danforth, Cooke & Co.'s No. 1095, built in 1879.

DENVER, MEMPHIS & ATLANTIC RY. succeeded the D.M.&A. Narrow Gauge Ry. organized in 1883; in 1891 it became part of the Kansas & Colorado Pacific Ry., controlled by the Missouri Pacific. It connected with the Pueblo & State Line R.R. and also had a line from Chetopa to Larned, Kansas. Eng. 4, the CHAUTAUQUA, built by Brooks in 1886, later became Missouri Pacific 986, and was renumbered 8723.

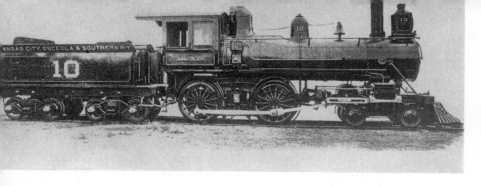

KANSAS CITY, OSCEOLA & SOUTH-ERN RY. Eng. 10 was named the JOHN I. BLAIR. Built by Cooke in 1894, she later became St. Louis & San Francisco's No. 44, later renumbered 94.

KANSAS CITY, FORT SCOTT & MEM-PHIS No. 109 was a 4-6-0 built by Pitts-burgh in 1890. Now a part of the Frisco system, the road linked Springfield, Mo., with Memphis, Tenn., and had lines in Kansas, Arkansas, and Indian Territory.

KANSAS CITY, WYANDOTTE & NORTH WESTERN'S Eng. 15 was built by Baldwin in 1889, Shop No. 9765. In 1893 the road became the Kansas City & Northwestern, controlled by the Missouri Pacific; Eng 15 carried the same num-ber on the KC&NW, later became Mo. Pac. 2735.
(Six photos, Collection of Dr. S. R. Wood)

OREGON SHORT LINE & UTAH NORTHERN Engine 589 is shown here at Pocatello Idaho, in 1889. Formerly OREGON SHORT LINE RAILWAY's No. 4, she was built by Grant in 1867 and rebuilt by Union Pacific.
(Henry R. Griffiths collection, courtesy of Arthur Petersen)

UTAH & NORTHERN Engine 759, taken at Dry Creek (now Dubois) Idaho, in 1888, shortly after the road had been widened to standard gauge. Built by Grant in 1870, the 4-4-0 had 18 x 16 inch cylinders, 63 inch drivers, and carried 150 pounds boiler pressure.
(Henry R. Griffiths collection, courtesy of Arthur Petersen)

UNION PACIFIC's No. 1012, a 4-6-0 used in yard service on the old UTAH & NORTHERN line at Lima, Montana, about 1890. Her stave pilot has been replaced by footboards for switching. She was built by Danforth, Cooke & Co. in 1880, originally UNION PACIFIC No. 209.
(Courtesy of Arthur Petersen)

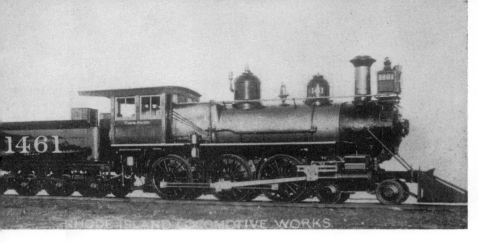

OREGON SHORT LINE & UTAH NORTHERN's Engine 1461 was a 4-6-0 with a Belpaire boiler built by Rhode Island Loco Works in 1890. She later became one of the 600 class on the Oregon Short Line Railroad.

(Courtesy of Arthur Petersen)

UNION PACIFIC's 1610 was a Cooke-built 2-8-0 used to boost freight tonnage over Sherman Hill, had 22 x 28 inch cylinders, 51 inch drivers, and were originally equipped with McConnell stacks. Fred Jukes shot the 1610 at Cheyenne in April, 1902. (Courtesy of Fred Jukes)

UNION PACIFIC 1621 and her sister, Eng. 1620, were Vauclain compounds built by Baldwin in 1900 with Vanderbilt fireboxes. Used on the Cheyenne-Laramie run over Sherman, they were not an unqualified success. The 1621 is shown at Laramie in 1902.

(Courtesy of Fred Jukes)

KANSAS CITY & OMAHA's second No. 33 was a 2-6-0 built by Rome in January, 1888, Shop No. 318. She later became BURLINGTON & MISSOURI RIVER's No. 433. Photo at Fairbury, Nebraska, in 1898. (Collection of Dr. S. R. Wood)

KANSAS CITY, PITTSBURG & GULF No. 25 was a Baldwin Mogul built in 1895, Shop No. 14434. She later was Kansas City Southern No. 304. Note the three-slot link and pin coupler on her pilot beam. (Collection of Dr. S. R. Wood)

CHICAGO, ROCK ISLAND & PACIFIC's Engine 332 was photographed at Eldon, Iowa, in 1885. Note the engineer's child on the pilot beam and his wife standing in the gangway of the trim 4-4-0. (Courtesy of Bernard Corbin)

Memories.

The American Standard locomotive, wooden cars, and wooden bridge in the sylvan setting are prophetic, for the waters of the flowing stream are trackless and wood is perishable before the ravages of Time. In the golden sunlight of happy yesteryears these symbols of Western railroading pause for a moment on Washington's Monte Cristo Railway bridge over the Stillaguamish River while the lens is uncapped and the image frozen for posterity. Look well, yet not sadly, for the era will live forever in the hearts of those who cherish the Iron Horse.

(E. J. McClanahan collection, courtesy of Fred Jukes)